# THE LITTLE BOOK

## OF

# REAL ESTATE
# INVESTING
# IN CANADA

# *Little Book Big Profits* Series

In the *Little Book Big Profits* series, the brightest icons in the financial world write on topics that range from tried-and-true investment strategies to tomorrow's new trends. Each book offers a unique perspective on investing, allowing the reader to pick and choose from the very best in investment advice today.

Books in the *Little Book Big Profits* series include:

# THE LITTLE BOOK

## OF

# REAL ESTATE
# INVESTING
# IN CANADA

## Don R. Campbell

**WILEY**

John Wiley & Sons Canada, Ltd.

***Library and Archives Canada Cataloguing in Publication Data:***

Campbell, Don R.
    The little book of real estate investing in Canada / Don R. Campbell.

Issued also in electronic formats.
ISBN 978-1-118-46410-6

    1. Real estate investment—Canada.   I. Title.

HD316.5.C34 2013          332.63′240971          C2012-907956-1
ISBN 978-1-118-46476-2 (ebk); 978-1-118-46474-8 (ebk); 978-1-118-46475-5 (ebk)

Printed in Canada

1 2 3 4 5 DP 16 15 14 13 12

# Contents

# Foreword

## *By Patrick Francey*
## *Sept. 2012*

— ❧ —

IT IS OFTEN only in hindsight that we are able to understand the true impact of a single decision. This is certainly true in my case, as there was no way I could have known the chain of events my seemingly simple decision to invest in real estate would set in motion. It is only now, more than ten years later, that I can see the obvious significance of that decision on me, my business, and ultimately my family's lives.

In late 1999, after 15 years as a small business owner, my wife Steffany and I decided it was time to expand our strategy for building our long-term financial foundation. Guided by the success and advice of friends and business associates, we chose to include real estate as part of our strategy.

After coming across a small ad buried at the back of our local newspaper inviting us to learn about Alberta real estate, we registered for our first-ever "real estate investing" presentation. It was being hosted by an organization called the Real Estate Investment Network (REIN™).

We had no idea what to expect, but were intrigued when speakers began to talk about the philosophy of investing in real estate. They outlined a straightforward, common-sense framework for using proven and key economic fundamentals that drive real estate prices to determine where to purchase investment properties. We were shown how, by considering and analyzing specific economic indicators, we could open a window to the future of specific geographic regions and neighborhoods, and see which ones made sense to invest in.

The good news was that the research and analysis clearly showed that at least 10 cities and towns in Alberta had economic fundamentals that supported a decision for investing in real estate. The even better news was that Edmonton was at, or very near the top of the list, and that is where we were living.

It was just a few weeks later that we attended a second REIN event, currently referred to as the Authentic Canadian Real Estate (ACRE) workshop. Over the course of two very content-rich days, a quirky, intellectual, and very passionate guy by the name of Don R. Campbell commanded the stage as he led the audience of over four hundred individuals step-by-step through a set of common-sense strategies and systems for successfully building a portfolio of buy and hold, positive cash flow, real estate.

What Steffany and I observed throughout the two-day event was that the foundation of Don's message was crystal clear: Treat real estate investing like a business, purchase property in areas where the economic fundamentals support the greatest possibility for equity appreciation, and only buy properties that produce monthly net cash flow.

Attending the ACRE weekend in 2001 turned out to be a milestone event in our lives as it was at that event we decided to step outside our comfort zone, become members of the REIN community, and begin to invest in real estate.

It was during our first few years as members, through interesting coincidences and combined with fortunate timing, that Steffany and I got to know Don and his wife Connie and we became good friends. During that same period of time, my other business interests had developed to a point where I was not required as part of the day-to-day operations of them, and so amongst the four of us the idea was born for me to join the REIN senior management team, which I did in January 2008.

With strategies and philosophies proven over 25 years of building his personal real estate portfolio and immersing himself in the experiences of a national community of other investors, Don R. Campbell continues to challenge us to view the world of real estate investing through the lens of creating long-term sustainable wealth. He stands out as a pioneer in providing real estate investors world-class research, education, analysis and leadership. Whether it's through the books he has written, REIN's monthly workshops and keynotes, or the many radio, TV, or newspaper interviews he does every year, Don continues to share his message, methodology, and strategies for others to successfully invest, not speculate, in real estate.

As REIN now celebrates its 20th anniversary, Don and our team remain steadfast in making a difference and continuing to create the conditions for success for committed real estate investors. Over the years we have received hundreds of handwritten notes, thank you cards and e-mails from members describing the positive impact Don and REIN have had on their lives. Being a catalyst for change in people's financial future and the success stories we receive fuel our passion to continually develop meaningful ways to improve ourselves and remain Canada's top resource centre for real estate investors.

Driven by the idea of investing, not speculating, in real estate, Don continues to expand his knowledge and the brain trust of people he surrounds himself with. Supporting real estate investors in reaching their highest potentials remains a core value of Don personally and of our team as a whole.

This "little book" is a powerful illustration of how some of our greatest successes and highest returns can be gained through investing in personal knowledge and education. Like his other books, this one continues to expand upon the insightful and common sense approach to investing in real estate that Don applies and teaches. For anyone interested in building a portfolio of investment real estate, this book requires a minimal investment but offers the possibilities of an infinite return on your investment—in yourself.

As for Steffany and I, leveraging the education, knowledge and expertise that Don R. Campbell and a national organization of real estate investors offer changed our lives. It too may prove to be your milestone decision.

**Patrick Francey**
**CEO**
**Real Estate Investment Network**

# Acknowledgements

⁓

LIFE, BUSINESS AND REAL ESTATE are never as much fun or as successful unless they are shared with great people.

This book is the culmination of 20-plus years of discoveries, successes, mistakes and experiences. It would be impossible to acknowledge everyone who has contributed to it without transforming *The Little Book...* into *The Massive Book of Real Estate Investing.* However, I would be remiss if I didn't mention a few key people.

None of this journey would have been possible without my wife of more than 25 years, Connie J. Campbell (www.conniejcampbell.com). She is the solid foundation upon which this life has been built. Her passion for life, her belief in me and her amazing business talents have helped our business grow to a world-class level. Without her this journey would have been average; with her it has been extraordinary.

The members of the Real Estate Investment Network (www.reincanada.com) community past, present and future are the reason I continually raise the bar in all areas of my life. Over the last 20 years, I have learned as much by helping them as they have learned by being members of REIN. The next 20 years promise to be an even more exciting journey together.

I can't say thank you enough to the REIN office team (all 27 of them). Led by Patrick Francey and Richard Dolan, they play at a world-class level and enable me to make a significantly positive impact on discussions about entrepreneurship and real estate investment far beyond Canada's borders.

A special thank you goes out to those who have questioned the validity of our research as well as our motives, and to those who just refuse to believe that our business is based on creating a community in which we all help one another. These naysayers fuel my passion to ensure our research is first-class and unbiased. By forcing us to answer tough questions, these people have forged widespread recognition of REIN as one of the market's most rational and trusted leaders.

The completion of this book would never have occurred without the talented Joy Gregory and Don Loney. Working with them since 2004 has been both a pleasure and an amazing learning opportunity. Without them, my ideas would not be articulated as clearly as they are and therefore would not have the impact they have.

Finally, a big thank you goes to all who use our research and investment strategies to create financial success for themselves and their families. You are the reason we continue to do what we do. Your successes are the rocket fuel that powers me forward.

Thank you all!

Don R. Campbell
www.DonRCampbell.com

# Introduction

~

IT'S A FEW MINUTES past seven o'clock and I'm at the back of the room at a REIN™ event. Patrick Francey, C.E.O. of REIN, is on the stage, opening the program. I take in the room—about 500 investors who are quietly creating their financial independence in the Canadian real estate market. Imagine that! Behind the bad news headlines of eurozone economic woes, a jobless U.S. workforce and the constant noise about where real estate markets are headed in Canada (which bubble will be the first to burst?), is a group of sophisticated investors hanging on to their financial goals. In fact, many of them are telling me that despite investing for more than 20 years, there has never been a better time to invest in long-term positive-cash flowing Canadian real estate. And I agree with them, but only in certain markets.

They are not crazy—and neither am I. I am not in the bullish or the bearish camp. I am pragmatic, neither a blind optimist nor a pessimist, and I am definitely not conflicted about my message. So let me be clear: when it comes to investing in your future, I really do believe that today is the perfect day to start whether in smooth economic waters or turmoil.

Being a pragmatist, I am not telling you to quit your day job, cash in every stock you own or leverage your family home to access a line of credit you can use to buy the first piece of real estate you come across on today's market. (An important disclaimer here: I will not now or ever try to sell you on the merits of a particular piece of investment property.) But I am telling you that real estate investment makes sense. It made sense 25 years ago when I bought my first investment property, and it still makes sense today.

## The REIN Connection

Let me explain why I am so confident. A lot of Canadians know me as "that real estate guy." They hear me on the radio or see me on TV and they recognize my voice and face. Some of them know that I am a founding partner of a national organization called the Real Estate Investment Network™ Ltd., more commonly known as REIN. I got involved with REIN 20 years ago. This relationship is critical to my story—and to my lasting enthusiasm for this particular asset class. But my real estate investment story does not begin with REIN.

By the time REIN came into my life, I had already invested in Canadian real estate, and looking back, I do wish that REIN had been in my life from the first property purchase onwards. In its earliest days, REIN was a pretty small organization, and I liked the fact that hanging out with this group of investors gave me access to what felt like rather exclusive opportunities to talk about real estate investment with like-minded individuals. Some of these people had already amassed impressive hands-on expertise thanks to the success of their own portfolios. Imagine what that was like for a guy like me! I was not yet a real estate investment "insider," but I was honing my investment skills, strategies and systems by surrounding myself with people who were fully immersed in investment real estate. The environment we wanted to create in REIN gelled quickly as those of us involved started to improve our results and reduce our risks by leveraging each other's experiences.

That early REIN experience became the catalyst for everything else I did in business. Building an atmosphere of collaboration, and openly sharing secrets, strategies and contacts—all the while providing amazing value for the members' dollar—were and remain the foundational elements of REIN.

Back then, the real estate education industry was far from cohesive and it definitely was not based on the philosophy we have since adopted. While I genuinely liked what I was learning from my REIN counterparts, in a lot of cases I also worked with investors outside of the organization. There I discovered a lot of activities and people whose underlying motives were suspect. These individuals were teaching business models that simply could not be sustained. These experiences to this day inspire the REIN team to stay focused on the business plan we established: help many and in return, you, too, get helped along the way.

I knew that you didn't have to take advantage of people's naivety, greed or desperation in order to have a long-term profitable business that also made a difference in the community. In the field of real estate investment education, there are promoters out to make a lot of fast cash for themselves while simultaneously generating lasting pain for a high percentage of their clients.

With my own portfolio growing along with values that were strong and sustainable, my wife Connie and I assumed full control of REIN in 2001 as the others retired. We made it our focus to make sure that this organization stayed far away from the shark-like promoters whose business models were all about separating honest people from their hard-earned money. As with most businesses, we made mistakes. We worked with some people we continue to respect today and with others whose influence was detrimental to the positive impact REIN was generating.

I am pleased to say that REIN stayed the course—and Canadians took note. Since 1992, REIN has grown from a British Columbia-based organization with a few dozen active members to a national association with more than 3,400 members. Right now, it is also being launched internationally. Thanks to its focus on teaching members how to buy and sell real estate to create long-term wealth, REIN members have secured more than $4 billion of Canadian real estate. None of that real estate is connected to REIN, the organization, because we do not sell property to our members. What we do continue to offer is a safe place to learn, access to exclusive research and direction on what tactics to use to profit in each segment of the changing economic cycle. Many of our members attend evening workshops once a month, plus all-day workshops every three months or so. Those who can't make it to these events automatically receive full digital recordings of the proceedings. They come out regularly because they see these gatherings as a chance to learn, to meet like-minded investors and to stay ahead of market trends.

Internet access has also helped us to find new ways to help investors. In addition to hosting valuable members-only market research data on REIN's website, we also post templates for all of the documents a strategic investor—either rookie or veteran—needs.

If you want to see what a first-class joint-venture agreement looks like, or peruse the details of a professional statement of accounts, just click your way to my blog at www.DonRCampbell.com and discover the latest Canadian, U.S. and international market research. Those are good examples of the kind of hands-on business tools REIN membership delivers.

REIN *relationships* are also critical. It is not uncommon for me to attend a REIN event and overhear snatches of enthusiastic conversations that include comments such as: "That happened to me, too. Here's what I did…" or "Do you know who I should talk to about that contract/that property manager/that neighbourhood?" I love it!

In addition to the relationships that investors build by participating in REIN, REIN's market research and analysis is second-to-none in the Canadian real estate industry. It is used by media, industry groups, cities and investors across the country. That unbiased data really sets REIN apart. Because it is market-driven and geographically applicable, this information helps members make well-informed decisions about the real estate investments they buy, sell or hold to generate long-term wealth. Do you need to know more about how a new transportation route in Vancouver or Hamilton might impact real estate values in certain neighbourhoods? Check out REIN's website. Do you want to know more about how the oil sands development might affects housing prices in Edmonton or Saskatoon? Those are the types of questions that strategic investors need to have answered, even if they don't know it when they begin. Best of all, REIN doesn't propose a thesis and then search for the data to support it. We let the actual data lead us to the conclusion, be it good or bad.

## Good Answers to Tough Questions

Without proper, unbiased information, an investor is really just a speculator. That's precisely why this book is so timely, especially given the turmoil that continues to disrupt the world's economy. *The Little Book of Real Estate Investing in Canada* summarizes a sophisticated approach to real estate investing. "Sophisticated" does not mean "complicated." On the contrary, I am a huge proponent of the Authentic Canadian Real Estate (ACRE) system. Backed by two decades of field experience, the ACRE system is all about learning how to do things right and then doing them right, again and again.

———————————— ~ ————————————

**I would never tell you that real estate investment is easy. I can assure you that it is a learned skill—and that those who learn to do it well can expect success.**

To help you understand what I mean by a sophisticated approach to real estate investing, this book follows a very specific path. Those who already own investment property will be able to read this book and then review their portfolios, business strategies and goals with a fresh perspective on what they should do next, or do differently given a changing market. And many newcomers will find that the book encapsulates the basics so that they will be able to move with confidence towards buying their first piece of real estate investment property. Here is a synopsis of what the book covers:

- **Chapter One: Why Invest in Real Estate?** takes readers through the basics of why real estate investing makes sense as part of a long-term financial plan. It begins with how I was introduced to real estate investing and shows readers how they can move towards those first discussions about making real estate investment part of their strategy to generate wealth.
- **Chapter Two: My Early Years as an Investor** looks at my earliest wins and losses. This is probably a good

time to tell you that I am a huge music and sports fan, which is why I often use song titles and sports analogies to summarize or make sense of my business choices. So bear with me! I really think it helps investors to find creative ways to think about business. Because I am the consummate business guy, I never lose sight of the fact that the dollars and cents of my decisions always matter. To put it another way, I take full responsibility for where the buck stops. But if a song title helps me capture the essence of what is or is not working in a business or personal situation, that title can also help me reframe the problem en route to a lasting solution.

The same goes for my relationship with sports. I do not shy away from the notion of winners and losers, and I know which side of the score sheet I want to be on. When troubled by a particular business snag, it sometimes helps me to shift into the realm of sports. Again, it is an issue of creative reframing and deliberately finding a fresh perspective. This cognitive approach helps me to see how my inability to hit a home run, for example, may have started in the dugout, long before I stepped up to bat.

- **Chapter Three: Design a Portfolio to Weather the Inevitable Storms** outlines exactly what that phrase implies. I have been able to avoid a lot of the mistakes investors make. This is not because I was smarter. I avoided certain landmines by virtue of the fact that I followed a system. In fact, I can trace all of the mistakes I've made back to the moment when I veered away from the system. It is as simple as that.

- **Chapter Four: Building the Team** examines why I make such a big deal out of never (ever!) letting myself think that I am able to invest on my own. I may be the master of my own destiny and the captain of my investment and business teams, but there is a team—and without that team, I am sunk.

- **Chapter Five: The Investor Mentality** targets an area that too many investors overlook. It is one thing to say you want to be an investor; it is much more difficult to actually be one—rather than a speculator. During the last recession, I saw a lot of very nice people make some poor choices about their real estate investment portfolios. I do not blame the economic collapse for their economic woes; I do blame a lack of "investor mentality." Fear and greed are nasty taskmasters, but a healthy investor mentality can help investors avoid the problems that typically accompany these two powerful emotions. A positive investor mentality also protects sophisticated investors from the plagues wrought by the demons of self-doubt. Self-doubt clouds business judgment, leading individuals to lose faith in their investment systems. Instead of sticking to a plan that includes "emergency" options, self-doubters waste their time (and lose their money) trying to put out fires.

- **Chapter Six: Riding the Cycle to Long-Term Sustainable Wealth** combines some of my favourite investment topics including the beauty of leverage, the wisdom of experience and the value of quality market research. Believe it or not, you already know all the people you need to know to grow your portfolio so that it can support your long-term goals for wealth creation. What you may not know is how to put all of the pieces together to build a long-term portfolio designed to create sustainable wealth. That's okay, since the concepts involved are entirely teachable!

- **Chapter Seven: Why Do You Really and Truly Want to Invest in Real Estate?** revisits the underlying personal reason that you are investing in real estate. In this chapter you will be exposed to this topic from a different point of view: a fresh perspective that often takes people by surprise. As a real estate expert with decades of experience backing me up, I can tell you why it makes long-term financial sense to invest in real estate. But I cannot tell you why *you* should invest in real estate, because this is something you must discover for yourself.

Warning: personal and professional goal-setting can lead individuals to a new and better understanding of who they are and who they want to be. In sum, Chapter Seven may knock your socks off!

- **Chapter Eight: Is Real Estate Investing Part of Your Journey?** sums up the key lessons of this book with an overview of what strategic investors must do to stay the course and avoid the minefields of misinformation and the distractions of fear and greed. Success demands informed action—and that's exactly what a proven system can deliver.

Again, I want to welcome you to *The Little Book of Real Estate Investing in Canada*. I have read a lot of business how-to books that left me wondering what they were really trying to tell me. That will not happen to you with this book. I promise to be straightforward (sometimes brutally so). You have questions about how real estate investment works in Canada and I want to answer them—and more. This little book can't tell you everything you need to know. It does tell you what you *most* need to know.

I know thousands of Canadians who got their start in this business by buying a single revenue property. I know what real estate investing has done for them and I know what it can do for you. You just want the facts? Then that's perfect, because facts are all I've got!

# Chapter One

# Why Invest in Real Estate?

~

Have you ever listened to the song, *Times Like These*, by the Foo Fighters? It comes to mind when people ask me why I think real estate investment is a good idea. I have no trouble answering that question, but I sometimes think the people asking are a bit disappointed by my response. They want me to tell this great story about the very moment I *knew* real estate investment was for me—I want to talk about moving!

A story like the one they want to hear would likely include some pivotal moment, for example, the instant the sun hit a "For Sale" sign as I was driving down a residential street and I realized (with an overwhelming rush of emotion) that I could be buying properties and renting them out to people who needed a place to live, or fixing them up and selling them to people who needed a place to live. A story like that would evoke an epiphany of real estate awareness and would likely include some instant understanding of all of the investment principles I've come to hold dear—principles such as the importance of focusing on long-term wealth creation and the deliberate forging of mutually beneficial investment relationships. It would also have to include some specific ideas about how one could set up actual real estate investment *systems*, systems others could follow on their own path to success. Now that would be a story!

The reality of how I came to see real estate investment as a good strategy is less dramatic. It's also a better story, but not because it has moments of high and low drama or because I'm so darned interesting. The real story is better precisely because I am just like most other Canadians. And that's really important. I invest in real estate because I can make money in real estate and generate future financial security for my family, myself and my charities—and that's it. I started investing in real estate because I could. I keep investing because I can. It has never been about what I knew or who I knew or having a giant pot of money to start with. I had none of those advantages.

It has always been about a commitment to a long-term outlook and working hard to minimize risk while making my money work harder than I do—and I work very hard. Opportunity, like beauty, is in the eye of the beholder. Keeping that in mind, I open this discussion of the fundamentals by encouraging you to be on the lookout for two very different kinds of real estate investment advice or comment: the kind you'll get from the Armchair Authority, and the kind you'll get from those who practise the Final 30-Feet Rule.

## Beware the Armchair Authority

Before we study the fundamentals that sophisticated real estate investors use to determine whether a specific real estate investment makes sense, I want to acknowledge the three primary arguments real estate investment naysayers will use to convince you that real estate investment is a bad idea. They will tell you that:

1. Interest rates will rise rapidly and anyone in real estate will go broke in an instant.
2. The real estate market is in a bubble (or approaching same, or about to break same) or a depression.
3. Nothing good ever comes from having tenants.

I am living proof that even with all of that negativity around, you can do incredibly well if you know what you are doing. (Admittedly, if you do not know what you're doing, you can create major problems.) As we don't seem to be able to escape the naysayers, I'll tell you how you can use information to counter their negative outlook.

Prophets of doom exist in all market conditions and it's impossible to steer completely clear of them. They remind me of Goldilocks, who discovers that bears have sampled three bowls of porridge, and found that one is too hot, one is too cold and one is just right. The only problem with applying this analogy to real estate naysayers is that in real estate, even when these characters find a property that is just right, they'd still tell others that it was wrong— and they should go eat eggs instead! Their reputation for having a negative outlook is more important to them than reality! Some even wear a "bear" moniker proudly—and that is why you need to be aware of the danger posed by their misinformed opinions.

I think new investors (and anyone whose portfolio is weathering a market storm or is looking for market direction when all he can see is a horizon of dark clouds) should recognize the three negative arguments listed above as warning flags. They are flags signalling arguments that should be disregarded, and they are more common now than in past years thanks to the fact that the internet gives everyone with an opinion a chance to share it. My point is that while everyone is *exposed* to these arguments against real estate, the strategic investor arms himself with the tools to analyze what's right. When you need to make investment decisions, no one else's opinion really matters, not even mine. When confronted with negativity, my favourite response is to ask the naysayer, "What type of real estate experience do you have?" If the answer is none, or very little, you know you're listening to an Armchair Authority, not someone who knows what he or she is talking about.

## Seek Out the Experienced Investor

Now consider the opposite of the Armchair Authority— the realist. I learned, very early on, to only take advice from someone who has been very successful in what I want to be successful at. You'll notice I didn't just say relatively successful, and I'm also not talking about someone who got lucky in a hot market. I want to learn from, discover insights from and hear the good and bad side of the investment world from someone who has seen it all and knows how to respond to all market conditions.

To look at how this works in the real world, consider how everyone you bump into seems to have an opinion on the real estate market. *It's a bubble! There are too many condos! There are not enough condos! It's going to collapse! It's a great opportunity! It's better to rent than buy!* And so on. As I wrote this section I was sitting on the patio of the local Starbucks and I overheard a real estate conversation at the next table. I chuckled at the mistaken myths they were sharing—and was chagrined to realize that the speakers seemed to be making important decisions based on what I knew to be myths.

With commendable candour, one 20-something enthusiastically shared her opinions on real estate. In just five minutes she noted:

- "You won't believe the deal I can get on a time-share! For only $46,000 I get two weeks a year at *no charge*. That's like a free holiday every year! The rest of the year it is rented out. Too bad it isn't by a ski hill but the winter sun will be great, if I can get those weeks!"
- "Downtown Vancouver is not that expensive. My friend has a 380-square-foot condo and pays only $1,400 a month rent."
- "My friend really wants to get a place in the States because the dollar is so strong. I told him it was a great idea and that a bunch of us should pool our money and then share the profits because there is no tax as a Canadian down there."

They say enthusiasm is a virtue, no matter how misinformed the enthusiast is. I disagree. From the gist of the conversation it was clear that no one at that table had any experience with even one real estate transaction. This young woman's declarations were so positive that her friends (even those who were significantly older than her) were accepting them as real estate gospel. She made it clear that she hadn't ever bought a property, but she had read a "ton" about the topic so she knew how it works. I was astonished to hear them respond as if their comments were written on tablets of stone.

Although certainly not lacking in confidence, this greenhorn investor lacked first-hand knowledge. Missing this critical piece to the success puzzle made her confident declarations and opinions very dangerous.

You would be right to think that a few people talking about real estate don't present an insurmountable problem for others in the business or for those planning to start. We all have to find our way in the world and that usually includes making (and then learning from) a few mistakes. But this lack of knowledge can be very dangerous when the misinformation and opinions come from people who call themselves real estate experts.

The importance of paying attention only to real authorities was first driven home for me when I heard how veteran comedian Buddy Hackett told a young and upcoming comic how to deal with the mountains of advice that TV executives, promoters, friends and family will give her as she builds her comedy career. Buddy's advice was simple yet profound: "Listen politely, smile and allow them to feel helpful...then turn around and seek out and take advice only from those who have walked the final 30 feet."

What did he mean by the final 30 feet? When I heard the answer, I saved it and have used it ever since. To paraphrase, Hackett said:

---

**As a comic, only take advice from those who have walked the final and most important 30 feet from backstage to alone in front of a mic with nowhere to hide. Then, and only then, will you know the advice comes from reality and not theory. They'll understand the emotions, the work it takes to get it right. They'll have made the mistakes and created the laughs, not just read about how to do it.**

---

These words of wisdom can be applied to virtually any decision we face in life. Hackett's point was that the world is full of inexperienced pretenders who can and will steer you wrong. Some will be confident that their opinions are correct. Others won't care. Be careful to choose advisors who have the final 30-feet experience in real estate—and look for advisors who have chalked up decades of experience.

Now back to the conversation at Starbucks. I'm sure that young lady thought she was repeating truths; she wasn't deliberately misleading her companions. But without having bought, owned, managed or experienced a lot of real estate transactions in all market conditions, she truly lacked the final 30 feet of experience needed to advise others about the financial and emotional realities of what it's like to face tough investment decisions. Book theory, number analysis, charts and graphs are just theories and numbers if you haven't *done* what it really takes to be a successful investor. Veteran investors know there is no theory when you are in the trenches and making real-life decisions.

That is why Buddy Hackett's advice served me so well as I built my business and real estate portfolio into what it is today. By continually seeking out people who had already achieved what I wanted to achieve and who had solved the problems I wanted to solve, I could avoid the mistakes they'd made. I still let the inexperienced share their theories and opinions. But now I smile politely—and quickly move on. Apply this to your own real estate investment business by looking for people who understand what the fundamentals are all about!

## The One Thing Strategic Investors Agree On: Focus on Fundamentals

How could the foundation of all real estate success be based in something as boring and dry as fundamentals? What happened to the excitement of the big cheque, purchasing a property way under value or the quick flip that added a few thousand bucks into your pocket? The good news is these do happen; in fact they happen more often when investors shift their focus away from a get-rich-quick mentality to dry, boring and extremely profitable fundamentals. Once your focus shifts, the great deals that provide long-term financial stability to your life show up much more quickly. Hidden within them are some fast, big-profit deals. In other words you get the ultimate combo deal (without all the fat, sugar and salt)!

Is this how I made my real estate fortune? Well, certainly not at the beginning! At the start I made all the bad decisions that anyone could make. While I got lucky with a few investments, I admit to chasing quick profits without even understanding the true value of real estate investment and what it could provide in terms of future financial security.

I'm pleased to say that changed. As I "looked behind the curtain" for ways to make real estate more profitable, I worked with other successful investors to develop the Authentic Canadian Real Estate (ACRE) investment system. Thanks to that approach, it is much easier for new investors to discover that if you make real estate a bit more boring, it becomes *a lot* more profitable. That's because:

———————————————— ∽ ————————————————

**Following the ACRE system is just like walking in the footsteps of highly successful real estate investors who aren't trying to sell you on anything other than the fact that they are doing it and it will work for you. What a breath of fresh air that is if you happen to come across a misinformed Armchair Authority!**

In sum, the ACRE system gives me and other investors a proven pathway to real estate market investments through what REIN members call "fundamentals." We do this to help new and experienced investors make real estate investment decisions based on market realities, not emotions like fear or greed. The ACRE system acknowledges that real estate investment has inherent financial risks. It teaches sophisticated investors to mitigate those financial risks by letting the underlying economics of their target region tell them whether it is a good time to buy, sell or stay on the sidelines. These investor know that real estate market numbers have very little to do with the reality of how the market performs over the long term.

—————————————— ∾ ——————————————

**Those who follow the ACRE system tend to position their portfolios 18 to 24 months ahead of the market. Because they recognize impending shifts in the market cycle, they can make bold moves before others even know that markets are changing.**

———————————————————————————————

First and foremost, strategic investors buy properties that fit their portfolios in terms of price and geography. While the less-educated majority buys and sells its properties because of emotional reactions to media stories (probably based on some Armchair Authority's rant about interest rates or bubbles!), the savvy investor buys and sells based on the market realities of economic fundamentals. Because she knows that the market is in constant short-term motion, she focuses on her specific area's long-term profit potential, not on monthly market peaks and valleys.

Investors who react to these short-term ups and downs leave money on the table when they let fear force them to walk away from properties that fit their portfolios or when they sell properties too early because they're worried about tomorrow instead of focusing on today. At one time I also brought an almost day-trade-like mentality to the game. It was horrible. There were sleepless nights worrying about my debt load (even though it was on investment-grade real estate). I was distressed by what I had to do if a tenant left in the middle of the night (theorists had told me I should *expect* that to happen). I obsessed about whether the market was going to collapse again (because it had already done that three times before I even got into the market). Yikes!

I was an emotional wreck, because I *really* didn't know how to analyze a market, a property or a tenant. I was just following everyone else. What a mistake that turned out to be! The solution came when I started to change the people whom I was learning from, whom I started spending my time with and whose information I could take to the bank.

---

**The emotional investor lets fear and greed rule. He aims for perfection—and misses. The sophisticated investor keeps it real—and wins.**

---

SUCCESS IS NOT A STRAIGHT LINE

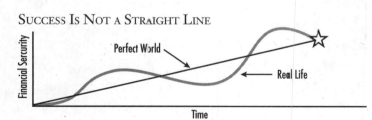

## Make Geography Part of Your System

Who would have thought so many years ago that economics and geography would be important to future financial wealth? All you hoped for was that your teacher didn't catch you napping in mid-afternoon class. I digress, but I do so with a point. Real estate investors need to understand the role of geography, but not location, location, location. While geography could be simply added to the list of top 10 fundamentals, the role of geography is so important that I always deal with it separately.

The first step to successful real estate investing is to look in a completely different direction than the mediocre majority. Your goal is to understand how to recognize regional economic strengths and then identify cities, towns or neighbourhoods within those regions that have a particularly bright future. We don't even look at the real estate numbers until after we have identified an area.

Using the ACRE system, the sophisticated investor looks for signs of future strength, not past economic success. Who cares about what's already happened? I'm investing now for what's going to happen in the future! Those who invest on past performance are chasing markets, which is a grave mistake. *Past performance is never indicative of future results*. Sophisticated investors equate that to buying a stock because its value increased over the last two years, or because the company used to be an economic powerhouse (see, for example, Nortel, Corel, etc.) They also liken that backwards-looking approach to market *speculation*—a polite way of saying "wishful thinking."

To identify regions that are poised for growth, sophisticated investors use the 10 economic fundamentals that will shortly be presented to you. They know that industrial development (energy developments, manufacturing plants, processing, ship-building, warehousing) fosters institutional expansion (corporate offices, health care, education). In turn, these lead to the development of commercial properties and to new and expanded transportation corridors, as well as to increased demand for the companies that support all of the people and systems needed to keep all of these economic wheels turning. At each and every step along the way, jobs are created and consumer confidence increases. In other words, with jobs you have a market; without jobs you have stagnation or worse, retraction.

---

**Job Growth = Population Growth = Rental Demand = Property Purchase Demand**

---

Real estate investors thus learn to listen for the news *behind* a new development. They ask:

- Where will that plant be built?
- How long will it take?

- Where will the construction crews live?
- Where will they work when this project ends?
- Where will the new plant's labour force find housing?
- How will those employees get to work?
- How might that affect where they live?
- What are the long-term prospects of this new venture?

---

### Just the Facts

- Residential properties located within 800 metres of light rail or rapid transit stations typically can charge rents that are 5 to 11 per cent higher than the prevailing market.
- National stats mean nothing to the sophisticated real estate investor. The fact that prices are up 5 per cent across the country means nothing in a city where they've dropped 5 per cent—or have risen by 8 per cent. Ignore national stats. Focus on your chosen geographic zone.

---

## The 10 Fundamentals of Successful Real Estate Investing

Once investors identify the geographic area they want to focus on, they need information that ensures they are well informed. Let's use a concept of a vault that stores information. These 10 fundamentals of successful real estate investing are like the keys to that vault.

As you read through each section, remember that sophisticated investors use these fundamentals to unlock the details they need to decide if a city, town or neighbourhood has a future. Each of these keys gives you specific information to predict whether and where real estate prices can be expected to rise or fall. None of them will tell you how much prices will vary. That's information the less-educated investor chases because he forgets that real estate investment is about long-term wealth creation. Successful investors, who are in it for the long haul, use information to manage the risk.

## 1. Mortgage Interest Rates

Canadians love talking about interest rates. What will the banks do today? Will the government finally start raising/lowering rates? Will the housing market boom/bust when the rates skyrocket? And so on. The problem is that few understand the complex interaction between interest rates and the housing market. Most believe that there is an inverse proportional relationship: interest rates go up, ergo real estate markets go down. This is not true.

Yes, interest rates do impact the affordability of a housing market, and when interest rates rise, home owners with a variable-rate mortgage will feel the crunch more quickly than those who are locked in. However, when you take the last 20-plus years and graph both the housing market percentage increase and the underlying Bank of Canada rate, you can see that interest rates play quite a minor role. Once again, math and statistics trump speculative talk.

We can't discount the psychological impact of a rise in interest rates. Announcements create frenzy in the market which eventually cools down as people try to get in before it is perceived to be too late. Then reality sets back in. In reality, interest rates rise and fall based mostly on the underlying economic strength of the country: hot economies generate hot job markets which generate hot real estate markets and inflation. When these occur, governments try to cool them off with an interest rate increase.

———————————— ∼ ————————————

**Investors who buy and hold real estate will benefit from interest rate increases because more people will stick with renting rather than buying, thus pushing vacancy rates down and rents up.**

Smart investors look for signs that will tell them the steepness of the rate changes and then make business decisions accordingly. By using information instead of conjecture, they mitigate risks and increase profits.

This makes low mortgage rates a neutral factor for real estate investors. Low rates help them to manage their expenses and accelerate their mortgage paydowns. However, if interest rates are too low, they also help more renters become homeowners. That increases vacancy rates, meaning investors might have to work harder to make sure their properties are full.

---

### Just the Facts

- An interest rate change to 5.25 from 5 per cent on a $100,000 mortgage adds $17 a month to your mortgage payment. If your investment property depends on that extra $204 a year to either make money or break even, it probably doesn't belong in your portfolio.

---

## 2. The Disposable Income Effect

Again, look for numbers that tell the real story. Increasing average income is the greatest indicator of the net wealth effect in a region.

—————————————— ∽ ——————————————

**If a town's average disposable income rises faster
than the provincial average, real estate prices
are poised to do the same.**

_____

That is why lower income tax regions often have higher
retail sales per capita. More disposable income creates
more jobs and builds consumer confidence. Consumer
confidence is then reflected in increased demand for real
estate. This correlation is why strategic investors look for
regions where retail sales and consumer confidence are up,
since they know it leads to a positive impact on the real
estate market.

Strategic investors use this fundamental to identify
potential real estate market movers before the real estate
market numbers show it happening. If the average income
is rising across an entire region (perhaps a province), look
for indications that it is rising faster in certain cities or
neighbourhoods.

The Disposable Income Effect also helps identify markets
that are overheated or filled with speculators (something to
avoid). Hint: if demand puts upward pressure on housing
prices without a corresponding increase in average income,
this strong increase is likely not sustainable. The community
may have short-term investment potential for certain real

estate investors, but it won't provide the long-term sustainable market or rental increases a strategic investor looks for.

## Just the Facts

- The Royal Bank of Canada produces a quarterly report on housing affordability (www.rbc.com/ economics). A well-balanced market for investors has a Housing Affordability Index of 33 per cent. That means it takes 33 per cent of pre-tax income to pay for a median piece of property.
- Sophisticated investors look for cities and towns in the 25 to 39 per cent range.
- Towns and cities above 39 per cent are most likely going to under-perform over the long term as they are overpriced relative to the ability for the citizens to afford it. If the market is +6 per cent over that range, you have identified a higher-risk market.

## 3. Increased Job Growth

Increased in-migration to a region, town or city is one of the most important indicators of long-term sustainable markets. It has and will continue to be the foundation from which an investor's business is built. With people you have demand (rental and purchase). Without a population increase, you either have a market filled with speculators chasing "cheap" deals or a market that is about to slip into negative territory.

This is an easy statistic to follow for your target region. Start by looking for news about people moving to your target area from other countries and other parts of Canada. Make sure they are moving there for jobs, not to retire.

## Just the Facts

- REIN's market research shows workers who relocate for jobs typically rent for three years before buying their own homes.
- Approximately 50 per cent of those relocated workers will keep renting, 40 per cent will buy and 10 per cent will move back out of the region.

## 4. The Real Estate Doppler Effect

At the macro level, this occurs when one city or town's economic windfall (e.g., a new manufacturing facility or plans to increase production and employee numbers) impacts nearby cities or towns. Housing demand first rises within the community most impacted. Demand lags but will eventually increase in nearby cities and towns as the main area becomes less affordable and "too busy" for locals.

Homebuyers and investors can also take advantage of the micro-Doppler Effect. It occurs in areas that surround economically-strong communities and in neighbourhoods near those being revitalized thanks to a new development (e.g., a new post-secondary campus or a healthcare facility). As in the macro example, the revitalized area's prices and demand jump first and then ripple out to the surrounding neighbourhoods.

## Just the Facts

- Write down six towns or outer suburbs where property values have not increased as rapidly as their neighbours that are closer to a particular economic hub. Find out what is happening with housing demand and prices in those outlying areas: both will likely begin to rise six months after prices increase in the more immediate area.

- Now look at neighbourhoods located near planned economic developments that are expected to or already have impacted housing demand. Has demand started to increase in these communities? Be mindful of the fact that older properties will increase faster than new ones and speculators tend to focus on new construction.

## 5. Local, Regional and Provincial Climates

Real estate investors make it their business to know what is going on with politics at both the macro and micro level. It is relatively easy to identify specific areas with strong economic growth, new jobs and an increased rental pool. Because "business friendly" equates to "real estate friendly," you also need to know what local and regional politicians are doing to support that environment. Look at taxation rates for income and property. What are the laws governing landlords and tenants? How difficult is it to change zoning requirements from single- to multi-family designations? Can you meet with individuals from the local economic development office to ask about their overall plan and expectations regarding pending or future developments?

This fundamental showcases the work sophisticated investors are prepared to do to help themselves understand their market. Organizations like REIN provide additional support with research data like its annual "Top Canadian Investment Towns" report. Researchers profile more than one hundred towns before narrowing it down to those poised to outperform the others!

Will every community in that report be ideal for every real estate investor? Obviously not. But these towns are the cream of the investment crop and studying a detailed report like this is a good way to hone in on the fundamentals of what you need to know before you invest.

## 6. Critical Infrastructure Expansion

The role of transportation hubs was touched on in earlier fundamentals. It merits its own category because it exudes opportunity for the astute real estate investor who wants to know why the economic fundamentals support investment.

When a major transportation improvement is announced, look for information about why it is necessary and who will benefit. Transportation is all about accessibility and accessibility is measured in minutes-to-work. Accessibility equals increased population. Increased population equals higher demand for housing. Higher demand for housing equals upward pressure on property values and lower vacancy rates.

Consider transit, highway and air traffic changes and then watch what happens after expansion begins. Remember that speculators will buy on the announcement. Smart investors wait until the work actually begins and after they research the implications of other market fundamentals. Those other market fundamentals include increased costs for labour and materials as a direct result of in-migration and infrastructure expansion. This increases the cost of new housing construction and renovation projects.

Increased wages also drive up rents and housing prices. Investors who focus on the existing stock of real estate can make these increases work for their portfolios.

———————— ∼ ————————

**What really matters is a working understanding of
how the market reacts to specific fundamentals.**

---

## Just the Facts

- Homes located within 800 metres of public transit stations will appreciate 12–15% more quickly than their market peers. Conversely, values decline more slowly if markets drop.
- Check out REIN research reports about the market impact of specific transportation projects, including detailed neighbourhood-by-neighbourhood analysis for the Vancouver area, GTA, Calgary, Edmonton and the Hamilton Tech Triangle.

## 7. Areas in Transition

Words such as "gentrification," "renewal" and "revitalization" signal fundamental economic shifts in the market value of specific neighbourhoods. Real estate investors wisely watch areas with gentrification potential because they realize these are the neighbourhoods people will want to live in as the renewal takes hold and properties are often more affordable than others in the city.

Revitalized neighbourhoods are wonderful places to purchase properties with good potential for value increases over and above the average for the city. But exercise caution: make sure the renewal is real and not a mere blip related to the announcement of a future development, be it private or public. Cash flow is often higher in these areas due to lower prices, but the tenant class may be variable. You don't want to be the first into one of these regions. The revitalization cycle can take a long time to take hold, especially if an announced development is delayed or cancelled. Wait and watch for real signs of revitalization: these include increased pride of ownership and increased demand.

Often you have to get over the reputation of a neighbourhood in these renewal areas. Remember when I mentioned earlier that a neighbourhood's past has very little bearing on what will happen in its future? An inability to grasp this point is why investors who live in or near these transition areas are likely to be the last ones to notice their potential. They can't get past a neighbourhood's bad reputation while those from outside the neighbourhood are able to view it with fresh eyes.

Revitalization, which truly begins one house at a time, often goes hand in hand with Fundamental 5, which involves political decisions regarding policing, community development and zoning. As communities gradually are transformed into places where more people want to live, investors will notice an increase in pride of ownership. Attracted by other economic fundamentals, new home-owners will move into the neighbourhood. As they start to upgrade exterior finishes and clean up yards, other neighbours will follow suit. More expensive cars will make their debut on driveways and in the street.

Sophisticated investors watch for signs of renewal combined with other economic fundamentals discussed in this chapter.

––––––––––––––––––––  ∼  ––––––––––––––––––––

**A tougher, more hands-on tenant profile often comes with investing in these areas of revitalization, so property management and proper renovations are key.**

With this negative comes the positive of higher value increases and more rapid rental increases relative to other parts of the city, a plus for long-term wealth creation.

Building on the connection between economic fundamentals, sophisticated investors realize that the Real Estate Doppler Effect works here, too. Communities next to neighbourhoods where revitalization is well underway often experience the same upward trend, but later down the timeline.

## The More Active Factors

The first seven fundamentals are often called "passive" fundamentals. Real estate investors need to understand how they work as they are instrumental to one's ability to focus on real estate located in a particular geographic area, but are out of the investor's control. Understanding the passive fundamentals help us assess economic strength. The next three fundamentals call for some serious work on the part of the investor. That's right. This is where the successful investor takes a property—and makes it better.

## 8. Creating Highest and Best Use

"Highest and Best Use" is a term that professional property appraisals often use to detail what a property could be used for if it was being used to its zoning potential. The concept helps investors in two ways. First, understanding highest and best use enables you to optimize a property's value. If the zoning calls for multi-family and it is only being used for single-family housing, the smart investor finds out what he or she needs to do to change that. Similarly, if it's zoned for commercial and residential but the top floor (residence) is not being rented out (or vice versa), the investor recognizes that as an active opportunity.

Second, sophisticated investors look at whether a property is actually performing to its highest and best use. They ask questions such as:

- What is the building used for?
- What might it be used for?

- Can it be converted to condominiums or rental units?
- Could the raw land be subdivided into separate plots?
- Is this single-family home ideally situated for student housing?

More importantly, they really understand the zoning bylaws of their target region, *plus* they understand if the city has plans to change the zoning. This information all comes from city hall. Only a small number of properties on the market will prove easy to change. Others may be possible, but only with expertise and funds. Zoning changes almost always merit a second look.

## Just the Facts

Be creative when it comes to determining highest and best use.

- Find out if you can rent out a garage separate from the dwelling without a zoning change.
- Put a coin-operated washer and dryer into multi-family rental unit.
- Can you charge more for parking?
- If the zoning allows basement suites, does the current homeowner have one?

- What is the potential for owning three adjacent properties and building a larger apartment building on them under new densification initiatives by the city?
- Is a university or college opening up or expanding nearby that will put upward demand on student housing?

## 9. Buy Wholesale, Sell Retail: Stratification

Real estate investors often think of the market in terms of their particular niche. Buy-and-hold investors buy properties to rent and keep them in their portfolio for five to seven years. Lease-to-own investors give renters a chance to buy the properties they rent, over time. The renovate-and-resell market sources properties located in high-demand neighbourhoods at bargain prices, then upgrades them for the resale market. Other investors, typically companies, buy properties at wholesale rates and sell them to investors or homeowners at retail prices.

These investors typically purchase larger multi-family properties such as apartment buildings. Armed with information about how they can rezone the property, they convert each apartment to an individual title. This is called "condominiumization" or "stratification." A similar process can also work with raw land, which is converted to individual lots to be sold at retail.

Stratification adds immediate value to each unit and can be extremely lucrative. But it takes deep pockets and quality legal expertise to make these deals work. I have witnessed many an unprepared investor take a heavy financial hit on properties they bought to stratify, only to learn the process costs more than they could afford or that the city has put a moratorium on conversions. Others have to hold properties for much longer than anticipated, not always a financially feasible option for individual investors.

What makes this a fundamental if these deals are so complicated? Successful stratification projects often have a ripple effect on neighbouring communities. Beautiful condominiums with professionally landscaped grounds also advance gentrification. So pay attention. Individual investors may not want to organize and finance an apartment condominiumization, but these projects often improve property values and increase rents in the surrounding neighbourhood.

## 10. Quality Proactive Marketing

Quality marketing is an economic fundamental that sophisticated real estate investors use to stand out from the crowd in a positive way. Proven marketing strategies attract the type of buyers, sellers, renters and money partners that add serious value to an investor's portfolio. These strategies also make it easier for them to operate their businesses because they provide ways to maximize income by minimizing purchase prices and maximizing selling prices.

To put that in terms of dollars and cents, real estate revenues, like any investment portfolio, are all about percentages. That's why investors take great care to make sure their marketing dollars are effectively spent. Since advertising is one of their main marketing costs, they calculate a gross return on investment (ROI) to ensure their ads are profitable. If not, they change them, making the message more compelling and effective.

## Calculating ROI

Cost of ad: $250

Number of calls: 9

Number of renters: 1

Months of lease: 12

Monthly rent: $850

Gross income from ad: $10,200 (12 months × $850)

**Gross ROI = $10,200/$250 = approximately 4,000 per cent[1]**

---

[1] By using this formula, the investor knows that every time the phone rang, the call was worth $1,133

Conversely, you don't want your ads to attract too many unfiltered calls. Answering questions that should have been answered in your ad wastes your time! What really matters is the *quality* of the potential renter or buyer who calls.

Of course, marketing is about more than advertising. Sophisticated investors know that every dollar they invest in a property needs to come back to them—times at least three. If your property can attract a 5 per cent rent premium over the current market, that equals $42.50 on a monthly rental rate of $850.

Your goal is to be at the top of the rental food chain— and to get there effectively and inexpensively. The real gravy comes when you choose your regions well (population growth, area of renewal *and* a new transit station within 800 metres of your property) and renovate the property to appeal to the more discerning renter (simple things like nice flooring, a feature wall and an updated bathroom). All of these factors can easily lead to you receiving 10 to 15 per cent above average market rents. In our example, that equals a minimum of $85 per month times 12 months. That's an extra $1,020 on your bottom line—just by being a smart marketer. Now take it a notch further and imagine you have 10 properties like this. Not bad! Over and above the positive cash flow you are already receiving, you're getting an extra $10,200 to do with what you like.

## Just the Facts

- Marketing is a science unto itself. Successful investors understand the importance of clearly communicating in all aspects of their business, and marketing plays a major role. Whether attracting capital to complete deals, going to a bank to get financing or attracting great tenants, mastering marketing is critical.

- These strategies are so important that we regularly discuss and share with our REIN members what works and what does not.

- Landlording Secrets—The Definitive Tenant and Property Management System, is a REIN home-study course that really focuses on marketing strategies for investors.

The 10 factors we've discussed drive real estate markets up and down. As you review them, you will see that they are often interconnected. The more of these factors your target region has in your favour, the less risk and more reward you can expect to receive. If there are only one or two factors in your favour, expect high risk and lots of real and potential headaches. Many factors? Well, that tells me you have identified a strong and long-term sustainable market that, even with the inevitable gyrations of the market, will serve you well.

Take the business section of your local daily newspaper and try to link as many fundamentals as you can to particular news stories. Each of these fundamentals has an economic impact on real estate markets. When they act in concert, they are especially powerful.

## The Pseudo-Fundamentals

I want to draw special attention to the importance of two investment strategies that masquerade as fundamentals. Their execution can be considered a sophisticated strategy. But more often than not, their execution is far from sophisticated. When people ask why real estate investment makes sense, these two pseudo-fundamentals merit thought— and caution.

## 1. Renovations and Sweat Equity

This is more of an investment strategy than an economic fundamental. Still, it operates as a fundamental because it can impact markets.

Let me explain. Many real estate investors get their start in the business by buying and renovating properties, which they then flip back onto the resale market. A plethora of television shows has helped promote this approach, and while it can work, investors must go into these projects with their eyes and ears wide open! To be honest, that doesn't happen nearly enough, which is why veteran investors view this part of the market with a certain amount of caution. They know it can work. That is, there is money to be made. They also know this segment of the market attracts a lot of first-time investors and a lot of speculators. That makes it a market segment dominated by inexperience and emotion. It is a strategy not to be followed without a proven system.

Success with the fixer-upper strategy is highly dependent on buying the right property, having the right trades ready and knowing a lot about marketing, renovations, economics and real estate. Those who do it well focus on well-built but somewhat neglected properties in neighbourhoods where the revitalization fundamental is already kicking into gear. These properties could also be located adjacent to neighbourhoods where demand is rising thanks to changes to transportation systems or economic developments that improve employment and wages. In other words, success depends on the strength of the 10 fundamentals. The more fundamentals a particular property has, the stronger its potential for the fix-and-resell market.

Investors who make this strategy part of their real estate business know not to mix these transactions in the same company as their long-term rentals. The short-term flips are treated as income for tax purposes, while long-term holds are more likely to be considered capital gains if they are ever sold in the future. Mixing them can lead to you losing the capital gains tax savings, if you are not careful.

Success in this renovation-and-flip market segment demands honesty. The investors must be honest with themselves about the first 10 market fundamentals, honest about how much renovations really cost, honest about the price they'll get when they sell and honest about a Plan B if the property *doesn't* sell.

---

**Because inexperienced and emotional investors tend to overestimate their final selling price and underestimate the real cost of the renovations, this strategy is fraught with trouble for beginners.**

---

If you're thinking of fixing and flipping, make sure you first get good advice. Learn how to keep these projects simple by finding properties that need cosmetic changes, not structural improvements. It can be done well and profitably. If not done well, it can cost you your business.

## Just the Facts

- Talk to your tax professional before you launch a renovate-and-resell deal. Properties bought for a long-term buy-hold-rent strategy are usually taxed as capital gains (i.e., only 50 per cent of the profit is taxed at your tax rate). Under Canada Revenue Agency (CRA) rules, profits made with the renovate-and-resell strategy will be taxed fully as business income. That's on 100 per cent of the profit (not 50 per cent).

- Property in this category can also be deemed as inventory. This provides the potential for the CRA to disallow the carrying costs of the property while you renovated it, meaning you cannot write off mortgage interest or any other carrying cost. Ouch! That doesn't make the deal untouchable, but it can give it a substantially less profitable bottom line. Get great tax advice before you take action!

## 2. Speculation

This investment strategy also masquerades as an economic fundamental by focusing on the myth of the great deal. Since speculation implies exclusive information, it often defies the truths of the first 10 fundamentals. The problem is that the information investors act upon is often based on gossip (at best) and on misinformation (at worst)! For example, good news stories like announcement of the 2010 Vancouver Olympics definitely helped some speculators make money in that region when they bought ahead of the crowd. The opposite happened in Hamilton where speculators bought properties based on the proposed location of a new stadium—and lost that money when the stadium wasn't built.

There is no question that speculators with quick access to cash are often able to jump in and buy property at great prices when they act on insider or just-released news of a major economic development. In cases where the development proceeds, these investors can make a lot of money. But let me be clear about the fact that this kind of purchase does not make them real estate investors, as such. It makes them speculators. Lucky speculators.

Speculation is not part of the ACRE system. All 10 of the economic fundamentals discussed, from critical infrastructure improvements, to interest rates, in-migration, the net wealth effect and quality marketing, etc., comprise a basket of market fundamentals that investors can analyze to help them build long-term wealth. In contrast, speculation is all about rolling the dice. Sometimes it works and many times it doesn't. A strategic investor always looks at ways to reduce risk and increase returns.

## Just the Facts

- Successful real estate investors evolve with education and experience. They learn to look for clues in all the right places. Always seek out business and political information that makes your business stronger. Join an investment network and look for ways to learn from success.

## Closing Deals, Making Money

Why does real estate investing make sense? Because it can be predictable, long term and provide regular income along with increases in net worth. But you have to follow a system and you must pay attention to real estate numbers and the important fundamentals that will tell you where those numbers are headed.

When I started investing in real estate, I knew very little about the market. But I dove in and became a voracious learner. Once I knew the useful tips and basic strategies, I jumped in deeper and built my portfolio, making some mistakes along the way and learning to minimize risks and increase profits. But it all started with nothing. Which is why I am so confident that successful real estate investment is a learned skill and why the ACRE system exists for investors. I sure wish I had it when I was starting out.

Now that the foundation is laid and you understand how to identify and analyze the market clues we call the economic fundamentals of real estate investing, hold on as we go back in time to look at what my earliest years as an investor were really like...

## Pocket Gold

Keep a copy of this Property Goldmine Scorecard in your car or on your smartphone and use it to practise the fundamentals of property analysis. This is the kind of due-diligence tool investors use to help them gauge the economic fundamentals of a particular property.

REAL ESTATE
INVESTMENT
NETWORK™
#1018, 105 – 150 Crowfoot Cres. NW, Calgary, Alberta T3G 3T2
*phone (403) 208-2722 fax (403) 241-6685 www.reincanada.com*

# Property Goldmine Score Card

Property Address: _____

Town: _____ Prov: _____
Source: _____ Tel:_____

## Property Specific Questions

☐ Can you **change the use** of the property?
☐ Can you buy it <u>substantially</u> **below retail market value**?
☐ Can you <u>substantially</u> **increase the current rents**?
☐ Can you do small **renovations** to <u>substantially</u> increase the value?

## Area's Economic Influences

☐ Is there an **overall increase in demand** in the area?
☐ Are there currently **sales over list price** in the area?
☐ Is there a noted **increase in labour and materials cost** in the area?
☐ Is there a lot of **speculative investment** in the area?
☐ Is it **an area in transition** – moving upwards in quality?
☐ Is there a major **transportation improvement** occurring nearby?
☐ Is it in an area that is going to benefit from the **Ripple Effect?**
☐ Is the property's area in **"Real Estate Spring or Summer?"**
☐ Has the **political leadership** created a "growth atmosphere?"
☐ Is area's **average income increasing** faster than provincial average?
☐ Is it an area that is attractive to **"Baby Boomers?"**
☐ Is the area **growing faster** than the provincial average?
☐ Are **interest rates** at historic lows and/or moving downward?

_____ = Total ✓'s

Does This Property Fit Your System?  ☐ yes ☐ no
Does It Take You Closer to Your Goal?  ☐ yes ☐ no

# Chapter Two

# My Early Years
# as an Investor

STING's *I WAS BROUGHT TO MY SENSES* always makes me
think about my early years as an investor. I have to say,
knowing what I know now about real estate investing,
technical real estate analysis, real estate cycles and the
importance of cash flow, I am almost embarrassed when I
look back to when I first started. I was so naive in the
ways of real estate: I didn't have a big support network or
research to draw from and I didn't really know how to

analyze a property. Yet here I stand today a successful investor who has lived through many a downturn and almost as many upturns. I stand with the scars, bumps and bruises collected along the way, and I'd say it really was all worth it.

I also believe my story could have been very different had I had known then what I know now and if I had a group of veterans to hang out with, like REIN members (I started investing long before REIN existed).

Like a lot of Canadian kids born in the 1960s, I grew up with the expectation that my life was going to be better than my parents' lives. And thanks to my parents, my youth was pretty good. My dad was the general manager of a Sears Canada store in British Columbia and my mom worked as a bookkeeper and office manager. We lived, along with my younger sister, on this great acreage near Abbotsford, which is where we moved from North Vancouver when I was in grade four. Life on the acreage-turned-hobby farm is where I developed my keen appreciation for the natural world (and for hard work). I must have had an eye for what made certain things valuable and that's probably why I collected stamps. I was also an entrepreneur: even back then I loved sharing my discoveries with others. I never made any real money selling my discoveries, stamps, vegetables or eggs, but I loved doing it and it certainly gave me a lot of practice talking and listening to people. As a young teen, I worked at neighbouring farms, and by age 16 I was left in charge of poultry and dairy farms when their owners took holidays.

In my early teens I also developed a passion for music. I became the go-to music guy for local parties. I still love music: to me it is the elixir of life. Looking back, I see that my musical tastes, much like my approach to business, were honed in the following two ways:

1. I was the contrarian. While my contemporaries rocked out to popular bands like Def Leppard, I was listening to The Who, Yes and alternative rockers like The Cure and The Smiths. This contrarian approach directly reflects my investment strategies today.

2. I know what pleases others. Hey, if I wanted to create the best musical atmosphere for a party, I paid close attention to the type of music they needed to have fun and then made sure they got that—even if it wasn't always my first choice.

I share this because anyone who's heard me speak has probably picked up on the fact that I really love music and I can often link very specific real estate memories to songs or albums. (I bought and wore out (yes, it was vinyl) the now iconic *90125* album by Yes while living in the first house I bought. Every time I hear a song from that album, I am transported back to that time and place.)

That appreciation for music and rock trivia also played a pivotal role in how I came to meet and fall in love with Connie. My sister, Joy Anderson, brought her by my apartment to meet my roommate, because Joy thought they would be a great match. Luckily for me he wasn't home, and the rest is truly history. That night was the first time we played Rock Trivia and I was amazed to discover that Connie was the only person I knew who could truly compete with me. So once again, music played a pivotal role in shaping my future. And 25-plus years later, I could never give the makers of that game enough thanks. But I digress. Let me get back to that real estate story and jump back in time a few years.

## Ownership Made Sense

I know that a lot of real estate investors get into property ownership because their parents are investors. Well, Dad worked for Sears and I started working at Sears when I graduated from high school—no real estate base there.

The real awakening of my real estate curiosity occurred very innocently while I was watching a Habs-versus-Leafs game on "Hockey Night in Canada." During the game, my friend's dad, Dan, began speaking about real estate and some of the things he was doing. It seemed random and out-of-the-blue because I knew him as a successful chicken farmer and had previously learned a lot from him about that. I thought I had a pretty good idea of why my parents worked so hard to buy the acreage where they lived: this property was a significant investment in their future. (As it turned out, that acreage was located in one of the most sought-after rural regions in B.C.'s Lower Mainland.) However, the discussion with Dan really shone a light on the importance of real estate as an asset class for creating long-term sustainable wealth.

At this point in my life, I knew that some people didn't own the homes they lived in, opting instead to pay good money to live in homes that other people owned. But knowing this hadn't taught me anything about real estate *investment*. Listening to my friend's dad talk was like listening to a veteran financial advisor. Until that night, I'd never given much thought to the idea that maybe I could (and should) buy homes for other people to live in and rent. It was obvious that it wasn't going to replace my income right away, but if this successful, grounded and knowledge-able man was willing to share his wisdom, I was willing to listen and learn. I was intrigued.

This conversation occurred in the 1980s, which were characterized by high interest rates, inflation issues and unemployment above 10 per cent. But at the time, I had no idea how important these factors were. All I knew was that real estate was going to be one of my "golden tickets" to financial success.

So, after a while, my "Hockey Night in Canada" friend, Daren, and I bought a property as a joint venture. And with that joint venture, the journey—with its bumps, bruises and scars—began. We knew nothing about macroeconomics, the analysis of a real estate cycle or even what our next move would be. All we knew was that we were in!

Was that a smart thing to do? In retrospect, maybe, maybe not. We didn't do it because we had a big master plan. We just knew real estate was the place to be. In reality, even if we wanted to learn more about real estate investing, the state of the Canadian industry was such that few resources existed. Most of the information that was available described quick flips and get-rich-quick schemes, which, at the time, looked very attractive given the absence of more sophisticated options. I was young and naive about a lot of things, but even then I knew that a fool and his money are soon parted by exaggerated claims of fast money!

So why did we do it? In all honesty, we were just taking what we'd learned from hard-working parents who walked the talk of fiscal responsibility. While some of our peers were out spending every dollar they earned, we were focused on a more contrarian approach (just like my music choices). We were not yet thinking in terms of long-term wealth creation. But we were, as Bachman Turner Overdrive sang, "Takin' Care of Business."

## Learning as I Went

Where did my real estate investments go from that first house? For a long time they went absolutely nowhere. And that's important to my story because I wasn't some kind of real estate investment prodigy: I didn't have a giant stash of cash that I could use to buy a bunch of properties. I was a working guy with a part-time job in a bargain centre where they discounted the furniture and the wages. That little fact matters because it says a lot about my early years as an investor. Forget the anecdotes of early successes and disasters—I nearly missed the whole game!

By the time Connie and I started dating (January 16, 1987), I was working full-time and had sold my share in that first property. Connie and I got married in December 1987 and we bought our first home in Edmonton in early 1989. I'd been transferred there with Conair Aviation, a British Columbia-based forest-firefighting company. We didn't even know what winter was until that first year together in Edmonton. Despite the weather—think minus-30 degrees (Centigrade) with a fierce wind the day we arrived—that move ignited our lifelong love of Alberta's capital city. And yes, when I look back on that experience, our understanding of Edmonton—and how it works and how it moves—definitely helped me develop a strong awareness of a residential real estate market that would get top billing in the portfolios of many Canadian investors by the mid-1990s and beyond.

The first home we owned as a couple was on 167th Street. We had driven back to Edmonton from Abbotsford and on that drive we listened to a complete set of *How to Invest in Real Estate* cassette tapes. That really shed some light on the path we were going to follow to make real estate an important part of our life. Although we certainly didn't understand our choice of property with the sophistication we could apply today, I do think we had this sense of that area as a neighbourhood in transition. Postwar Edmonton had weathered the economic and cultural changes of the 1960s and 1970s and the soul-crushing economic downturn of the early 1980s. It was beginning to be a positive place again, with that enthusiasm largely fuelled by job growth connected to the petroleum industry.

Houses similar to the one we bought needed work, but they had basement suites for rentals. And, because of the strengthening economy, the real estate market was also doing okay. So the hard work we put into the house paid off both while we lived there and much more when it came time to sell. The neighbourhood was safe and offered good access to the rest of the city—market characteristics I now talk about in terms of investment potential. Even though real estate was far from being our primary focus, we certainly understood that we wanted our mortgage payments to go towards a property that would hold its own, or appreciate.

From 167th street we moved to Lessard, a community on the west side of Edmonton. There we bought half of a beautiful duplex in a neighbourhood of large, newer homes that, at the time, were on the edge of the city. In fact, there was a canola field half-a-block west of us. I learned an important lesson here about buying one of the less desirable houses in a great neighbourhood: the values are protected! Indeed, a friend who was investing in real estate reminded me that as new homes were built, houses like ours would benefit from the appreciating values in those newer areas. He never called it the Real Estate Doppler Effect, but he obviously knew how to tap into that fundamental!

We were young, happily married and gainfully employed: our life in Edmonton was on an upward trajectory. I even moved jobs to become the general manager of a local aviation company. We thought we had it made. Life was great—and trending up.

In early 1992, a family friend, Alan Jacques, showed up in Edmonton to teach a financial course and we invited him to stay at our place. I was still in my twenties, and I boasted a little about the fact that the two owners were the only people in the company who were higher than me on that corporate totem pole. Connie and I were living in the second house we'd bought and I really felt like I was on top of the world—with a future that looked pretty darn good.

Imagine my surprise when Alan suggested that I was, perhaps, peaking a little early. He challenged me to think past what I was doing right now and to look at what I might be able to do in the future. I balked. I wasn't entirely averse to the idea that I might want to try new business ventures. But the thought that there could be more than this was a little other-worldly. Given where I was professionally, I felt that a move away from the aviation company would sacrifice security for destinations entirely unknown. Much as I knew and respected Alan, I couldn't help but wonder if he really knew what he was talking about. Keep in mind that we still weren't talking real estate so much as raw entrepreneurship.

Then I remembered that conversation in front of the Habs-and-Leafs game when I first got the message that sitting still is moving backwards. Alan was a catalyst of that thought change. This was another instance where exposure to the perspective from an outside source led to a breakthrough. I was learning the value of gathering new viewpoints—a practice I now use every day.

———————————— ❦ ————————————

**Life has taught me the wisdom of being open-minded and willing to listen to new ideas. You can't possibly follow every new idea that comes your way.**

## Perspective Brings New Reality

I try to pay attention to new ideas and different ways of seeing the world. Of course, it's not possible to follow through on every promising suggestion. You can't possibly act on every new idea that comes your way. Many people try that and end up broke, tired and frustrated. You also can't un-know what you learn. And that's why Alan's comments, along with my life experiences to that time, meant that the seed of a new perspective that Alan planted that afternoon grew into what we have today.

As that was going on, Connie learned her job with Air BC was about to lead to a transfer back to Vancouver. One of the factors that kept me from acting on Alan's plan was the fact that Connie and I needed a salary to live on if I branched off into the unknown. Her transfer led me to give up my job with SkyHarbour Aviation and helped us reframe our situation. Before long we were back in Vancouver, this time renting a leaky condominium while we searched for what's next.

Interestingly enough, moving from Edmonton to downtown Vancouver provided me with a fresh perspective on how supply and demand (not actual value) drive market prices. This was a time when buyers in Edmonton could get a small mansion for what you had to spend on a condo in Vancouver. That ratio has shifted, with demand in Edmonton based on job and population growth pushing up the values in that city. Still, it was a fantastic opportunity to learn that the actual dollar value of property is not as important as demand for property. This principle explains why the cheap property is not always a good deal.

It was around this time that I was enrolled in my first weekend-long transformational workshop. The workshop was designed to get participants to start thinking that they had the power to control a lot of their future, financially, as well as in terms of family and personal philosophy. As part of that workshop, I wrote my first formal life purpose statement, which today still hangs on my office wall:

> To use my humour, honesty and intelligence by reading, gaining knowledge from all sources, and keeping everyone around me in a positive frame of mind, so I create success in my business and all areas of my life so that everyone has everything they need to be comfortable and to enjoy their lives.

I won't pretend that I knew everything that mission statement was meant to encapsulate. I can tell you that when I looked back on that statement years later, I realized that it marked the first time I had thought about my life as having a purpose. More than anything, I believe that workshop helped me tap into a resource I'd always appreciated—and taken for granted. In a nutshell, it convinced me that there was great value in surrounding myself with people who were kind of like me. I valued humour, honesty and learning, and I liked being around others who valued the same things!

That workshop also gave me first-hand experience with how exciting it is to be around people who want to take control of their future in a way that helps others to do the same. For the first time in my life, I realized that the people I admired most were the people who took responsibility for their lives. None of them were negative. None of them played the victim—even though many could have done so, considering what they had been through.

———————————————— ∿ ————————————————

**I learned that we all have circumstances in our lives. Some use past experiences to hide behind and others use them as a catalyst for positive change.**

The people I met there understood that financial security was a key component of a healthy and secure future and to that end they were actively engaged in pursuing business ideas that could make that happen. But chasing the almighty dollar was not the reason we were born. I wasn't really sure what that meant for me. But I was excited—and a wee bit scared.

## Some Wins, Some Losses

I've met people who don't want to hear that real estate investing was ever scary to me. They want me to be That Guy. That Guy who never looks back. That Guy who always knew what he wanted and how to get it. That Guy who never makes mistakes. King Midas, but in real estate.

I was never That Guy. Like Richard McTavish, the protagonist of my first real estate investing book, *Real Estate Investing in Canada 2.0: Creating Wealth with the ACRE System*, I was a guy who worked hard and loved my family. Unlike Richard, I actually liked what I was doing for a living. Now that I had left the aviation world, my pay wasn't great but I loved what I was doing. Like Richard, I felt undeniably stuck even though I was going through the motions of moving ahead. I was the captain of my own ship—but I really didn't have a plan for where that ship was going.

And that's how my early efforts at entrepreneurship came to include a number of business ventures, some successful, some not. I launched a publishing firm. I worked as a printer broker. I looked for ways to add real economic value to other ventures. I taught, I learned, I pushed myself to never stagnate. The one constant (two if you count Connie—and I certainly do!) was that I continued to nurture my connection to other people like me: those who valued humour, honesty and intelligence and liked working with others to make good things happen.

## The Real Estate Connection

Over time, several members of this initial core entrepreneurial group acknowledged an important common denominator: interest in real estate investment. No matter what else we were doing in our entrepreneurial lives, we always talked about real estate. Some of us were investing in real estate. Others wanted in as money partners. Still others just longed to know more. This is the seed that grew to become the Real Estate Investment Network.

Like a lot of entrepreneurs who saw value in diversifying their investment portfolios, many of us had already bought and sold properties prior to joining an association of like-minded investors. When REIN was launched in 1993 by my long-time mentor Alan Jacques, I became a charter member. Unlike a lot of our real estate investment counterparts, however, our interest in investing led those in REIN to start collecting, comparing and analyzing solid information about what made some real estate investments fail, while others cash flowed and still others absolutely flourished. Some of the information we were amassing came from our own experiences. A whole lot more came from the people we were getting to know.

As we attempted to compile more accurate information and clear strategies, it became obvious that the real estate investment industry in Canada had a problem. Being a skeptic at heart and a realist in hand, it became a real issue when seeing that some of the industry's so-called mentors were incredibly great *sales* people, but they weren't mentors at all. Because many of these individuals profited from the ignorance, they had no real incentive to teach others how to successfully invest in real estate. (If they did that, their client base might disappear!)

That is how REIN tied very nicely into my life philosophy, which is that success in business comes through helping others to become successful. Everyone benefits by giving people plans, directions, strategies and information that gets them out of the financial impasse in which many people are trapped.

That's right. Real estate was about to become actually doable for the average Canadian. This approach lacked the sexy attention-grabbing promise of the get-rich-quick pitches. But it was quite obvious that those who understood the value of long-term sustainable wealth would be interested in this brand-new message and brand-new model.

---

**The Real Estate Investment Network set out to show investors the difference between real estate investing and real estate guessing.**

## REIN Takes Off!

The next few years were a whirlwind of activity. REIN was flourishing in British Columbia by the time I found myself back in Alberta helping to make REIN a success in that province. Before long, REIN was handing out Bronze Awards to members who had bought at least three properties. The first Gold Awards were granted a year later, this time to members with at least 17 properties in their portfolios. Ironically, it took me years to get to my third property because, remember, back then I was doing it on my own. The members, in essence, were kicking my butt in speed and quality!

Before long we were fielding calls from investors across the country, with most of the calls coming from British Columbia, Alberta and Ontario. These were provinces where people who owned their own homes were waking up to the idea that they could leverage that investment to create long-term wealth by investing in homes for other people. As well, both veteran and would-be investors were hearing stories about REIN's market research and the fact that members were using investor-developed systems to achieve success.

Looking back, it was the reputation of our unique and cutting-edge research, combined with our singular focus of not having constant sales pitches at our events, that prompted membership to really take off. As our data and analyses hit Canadian streets, they filled a void and REIN membership swelled to more than a thousand. Numbers like that allowed us to expand our research department, bringing in top economists, analysts and others willing to shed light on the reality of the real estate market. As success stimulated success, membership benefits skyrocketed.

Fuelled by the enthusiasm of other members, and enlightened by the research REIN provided, Connie and I were building our own portfolio. We were also proving the truth behind another life-affirming statement that hangs on my office wall. This statement, originally uttered by motivational guru Zig Ziglar still inspires me: "You can have anything in life you want, if you just help enough other people get what they want."

News of what REIN was helping Canadians do continued to spread. Growing numbers of investors and market analysts were attracted to what REIN offered and they brought their personal business stories to REIN functions. Expanding membership added value to the organization through the members' willingness to share their real-life stories: their mistakes, their wins and their contacts. Together, REIN staff and members were creating an organization far bigger than the sum of its parts. And this philosophy remains today. REIN has never been about the speaker on stage. It has always been about the information shared by all.

REIN was attracting individuals who were keen to exchange what they knew of real estate investment and that approach was laying a solid foundation making it possible to develop systems that could be put into place one day and improved upon the next.

In 2001, Connie and I took over the reins of REIN. While details of the organization's evolution are not as important as the success its members were creating, I must say their success led Connie and I to want to make it even stronger and deeper. So that became our focus: we ignored the naysayers and set out to do what we could to make a difference in as many people's lives as possible while continuing to build our own portfolio.

By 2001, the economic fundamentals were telling us that Alberta was on the cusp of something big in the real estate market. Emboldened by that data, Connie and I focused our investing attention right where the numbers told us to go. It was exactly what we were teaching the members and it wasn't just exciting, it was fulfilling. What we were teaching *worked*.

Learning tough lessons from seasoned investors who had made and lost money in the real estate market, I expanded our portfolio while staying true to the three most important principles of my system:

1. Cash flow is king.
2. Market appreciation is a bonus.
3. Following the economic data is the foundation to making great investment decisions.

I stand by these principles with pride. But let's be clear. While principles govern one's business practices, those principles must tie into an over-arching goal. Without this goal, it could easily be just about chasing money.

## Forecast: REIN and More REIN

When Connie and I assumed control of REIN in 2001, I took a hard look at what the organization was doing and analyzed where it matched my values. Where appropriate, I ever so slightly shifted the organization to make it even more effective for members. My daily interaction with REIN members, non-REIN investors and other industry insiders (including real estate agents, market analysts, lawyers and property managers) told me that investors and REIN members didn't want properties sold to them. They would rather come to REIN to learn to fish, rather than be handed the fish. I was delighted! What members wanted was an organization that fit my values, my life philosophy and my integrity better than I could have imagined.

A side story to this journey occurred in 1999 in the midst of these big business changes, when my dad began to have some major health problems. I remember that Connie and I were driving back from B.C. to Calgary after seeing him in the hospital when the song "The Living Years" by Mike & the Mechanics poured from the car's speakers. It was at that moment our life changed again. As we listened to those words of loss, Connie turned to me and asked why we didn't just move back to Abbotsford to take care of my mom and dad. In life, as in business, doing the right thing isn't necessarily the most logical course—but it often turns out for the best.

As part of that process of unpacking after the move, I came across a binder of information from that very first workshop back in 1992. For fun, I started to leaf through the pages and that's when I rediscovered the life philosophy statement I had written years earlier. It floored me to realize that, even though I had basically forgotten about that statement, my life had taken me to a place where I was now *living* this philosophy. That discovery could not have come at a better time: it coincided exactly with the completion of our analysis of the direction we wanted to take REIN. This was *perfect!* Connie's and my response to my dad's health crisis played a key role in turning REIN into what it is today. We weren't on a path we had stumbled upon: we were on a path we had *chosen.*

The subtle shifts in how REIN operates really helped differentiate the organization from others across the country. Did the decision to not offer real estate to members cost us millions? Absolutely it did. But I learned a long time ago that integrity and living up to your own values matters a lot more than money. This approach to REIN's business also allowed me to build my portfolio much more quickly than I thought possible. The bottom line is that staying true to my philosophy of helping others meant I left lots of money on one side of the table—and made lots of money on the other. Win-win.

More than a decade later, I wouldn't change any of that. If anything, I am even more committed to the idea that people can learn from the successes and failures of others. And I can say that because I believe that REIN has proven it.

## REIN'S Success

I was recently asked to summarize the most important things that REIN membership teaches. In terms of my own portfolio's success, I know that my interpretation of the role of cash flow, appreciation and win-win relationships has served me well. In terms of what I learn from REIN—and what others are still learning from REIN—my answer shifts to the bigger picture. Right now, those who focus on underlying economics are uniquely positioned to (contrarily!) drive through the continual bombardment of news, analysis and commentary that hits us all every day. I have to say that the sheer quantity of information, and its capacity to overwhelm and confuse us didn't exist in the 1980s when I started out, and it wasn't prevalent in the 1990s either. The massive amount of information now coming at investors is so great that many people get stuck in neutral. They take no action because they don't know if there are any ports in the storm. That condition of being stuck changes when these same individuals tap into REIN's resources. This is when the success curve gathers momentum. Today's contrarian is tomorrow's leader—and that is what REIN continues to be a catalyst for: creating market leaders.

Success, now more than ever, will be built on a platform of solid and unbiased research. When investors finally discover it, and they start to stand on this solid platform, they find their confidence growing. This protects their investments from the havoc wreaked by emotional swings—and their portfolios grow stronger and sturdier in the process.

As an added bonus, investors on that sturdy platform are surrounded by people who are serious about improving the way real estate investment in Canada is done. These people are not afraid to look behind the curtain of confusion generated by emotional responses to the biased and just plain bad information available. They look at real information and then act accordingly.

What kept me from making mistakes was the opportunity to stand on that sturdy platform and then share my discoveries with others who had been on the path I once walked blindly!

And that's why my answers to questions about REIN's lasting value push past my own portfolio. The principles of cash flow, appreciation and positive relationships with the people I work with are central to my portfolio's success. My involvement with REIN has allowed me to put those principles into strategic action for my business. But I practice those principles within the rules that I've come to think of as the Three Cardinal Rules of Successful Real Estate Investing. They are:

1. If you want to invest in real estate successfully, find others who've invested in real estate successfully.
2. This is a business, not a get-rich-quick scheme.
3. You can follow systems for success. There is no need to reinvent the wheel.

As you will see in the next chapter, I do not deviate from these rules: they keep my business focused on the economic fundamentals that help me make money. I am not in business to chase money. I invest in real estate to create long-term sustainable wealth for myself and my family.

## Pocket Gold

There are three essential components to successful real estate investment. They are:

1. Systems
2. Relationships
3. Follow-through

**Systems** are the foundation upon which you build your wealth.

**Relationships** fuel your business and make success possible. To be the best, surround yourself with the best.

**Follow-through** is all about action. Dreams are for dreamers. Results are for those who take action.

# Chapter Three

# Design a Portfolio to Weather the Inevitable Storms

KEANE IS ONE OF THOSE English alternative rock bands whose music makes me think. Their song, *Can't Stop Now,* is all about the way life keeps moving—even if *you* don't. Well, real estate investment markets don't stand still either. Investments of all types have risks and rewards; they all encounter cycles, booms and storms. Real estate is no different, although strategic investors do have a modicum of additional control. Believe it or not, that control begins with actions you take before you buy. The more you do before you invest, the better your ship will be able to ride out the storms. In most other investments, your control of results is limited. With real estate, much of the outcome is in your hands—as long as you follow a long-term investment system.

Before I get into what you need to do to develop a portfolio that can weather inevitable economic turbulence, it is important to acknowledge that we are investing in historically complicated economic times. I know that a lot of readers have some serious questions about real estate investing and, in fact, any type of investing in the aftermath of the 2008 downturn. I don't blame anyone for remaining fearful, especially if they lost a lot of money or their job, or know someone who has. Honest concern aside, it is important to note that many thousands of investors more than weathered this latest storm, despite the rocky conditions it created. They did this by creating income and increasing their asset base during the crisis and its aftermath.

When the U.S. economy collapsed in September of 2008, American real estate markets took massive hits as this downturn pushed their markets back to and even below where it should have been on the long-term trend line. Those who got hurt the worst were those who thought that real estate would truck on forever. "Up, Up and Away!" was their motto. Unfortunately, they didn't understand just how

over-priced the market was vis-à-vis the underlying softening of the world economy. Worse, that softening was accel-
erated with the banking crisis. Talk about the perfect storm!
All the negatives hit real estate markets at once. As a market
analyst whose view is shaped by my location north of the
49th parallel, I can honestly say that the collapse of the U.S.
economy from the credit crisis generated a global economic
collapse that few saw coming. During the run-up and fall-
out of this crisis, we kept an extra sharp eye on Canada's
economy and housing market. Putting the attention of our
research team solely on this important sequence of events
allowed us to shed some critical light on the issues for
REIN members.

Yes, we did take comfort in the knowledge that Canada's
highly-regulated banking and mortgage industries provide
Canadian consumers—and real estate investors—with some
systemic protection from widespread market speculation
and greed. However, we are never immune from world
events, and what happens in China, the United States or
Europe inevitably has effects on Canada, so keeping a close
eye on the world economy is important. Stocks dropped
sharply in both countries and real estate in many regions of
Canada took a short-term drop (thankfully nothing like the
States). We also saw that the regions (and stocks) that were
strong on fundamentals came back the most quickly. As
"supply versus demand" and "safe havens" became the

watchwords, speculation disappeared. In stock markets, a demand for dividend-producing stocks increased while properties that created their own monthly dividends (cash flow) also rebounded quickly.

And therein lies one of the biggest investment lessons investors could learn from 2008. In sum, *income* was the difference between those who made it through the storm and those who didn't. The real estate investors who survived financially didn't particularly enjoy the ride, but all of the preparation they did to carefully choose their target geographic regions and then focus on creating positive cash flow generated a stability others lacked.

------------------------------- ∼ -------------------------------

**Then, as now, income and cash flow formed the safe harbour that protects investors.**

---

From my position at the helm of REIN, it was easy to see that some Canadian investors were poorly positioned to ride out the economic upheavals of the post-2008 world, typically because they were caught up in this notion of continual value increases. Others got through safely by hunkering down. They made income a priority and aggressively marketed for quality renters. They focused on reducing operations costs, just as any other strategic business owner would do who faces similarly tough times.

In contrast, non-strategic investors let greed and fear master their decision-making processes. This approach often led to wide-scale losses when Canadian portfolios had to be dispersed to pay lenders or avoid the continued financial pain of negative cash flow. Others got out of the investment business because they couldn't handle how the financial stress compromised their personal and business relationships.

Strategic investors fared much better. While many of them admit to being surprised by the rapid market decline, given what was happening in much of the Canadian economy, few were caught completely off guard. Most of them were able to take a deep breath and face the rising seas of bad economic news head on. Their properties were well positioned for the long term and, because they weren't selling in a depressed market, they could focus on bringing in steady revenue.

For a better look at how to make that happen in your own portfolio, keep reading!

## Strength: From the Ground Up

Anyone who's ever looked at building codes knows that regulations are typically based on local conditions. If you are building in a hurricane, tornado or earthquake zone, the applicable code sets out specific rules. As I see it, the same principle applies to building a portfolio. You may launch that portfolio in clear skies, but you plan for the day when that portfolio has to weather an economic storm.

When I make comments like this in front of new investors, I tend to get a lot of nods. No one gets into this business to lose money—and who doesn't want a strong portfolio? But many aren't prepared to do the work it takes to build that strong foundation, especially when the economic skies and forecasts are all sunny. That's why it takes them by surprise when I then ask these investors to tell me what the 10 fundamentals of real estate investing (recapped below) *really* have in common.

1. Mortgage interest rates
2. The net wealth effect
3. Increased job growth and in-migration
4. The real estate Doppler effect
5. Local, regional and provincial political climate
6. Critical infrastructure expansion
7. Areas in transition
8. Creating highest and best use
9. Buy wholesale well retail: stratification
10. Quality marketing

At this point in the discussion, a lot of non-strategic investors are keen to talk profitability and long-term financial security. So they think my question is all about fishing for an obvious answer such as:

- The fundamentals are all about putting your money to work.
- Real estate investors use fundamentals to put passive income to work to generate long-term capital appreciation.
- Strategic investors use the fundamentals to mitigate risk. They know that it's easier to lose than make money and they are strategic in how they move forward.
- These fundamentals are the crux of a proven investment *system*.

After processing answers like that, I'm usually left wondering if anyone was listening! What I really want these newcomers to say is that the fundamentals help them *buy the right property*. How's that for simplicity?

## Buying the Right Property

There's an old adage that says hindsight is 20/20. In fact many pundits and commentators use 20/20 hindsight to make themselves look good. Sadly, many investors, both real estate and stock, use 20/20 hindsight to beat up themselves (and others) emotionally. *I should've bought more! I should've sold earlier! I wish I hadn't sold then!* These three statements of regret can be poisonous. Investors must understand that they will *never* time the market perfectly. It's normal to wish you had done more/less/nothing at some point of the cycle, so recognize that fact and keep moving.

---

**Your job as an investor is to study the fundamentals, analyze the actual property you are buying and then manage that property through all types of market conditions—not to out-guess the cycle.**

---

If I had waited for everything to be perfect, I would never have bought my first property and definitely not my one-hundred-and-seventy-first. That said, ignorance is not bliss and ignorance in business will cost you money. Ignorance leads to risky choices, risky choices lead to speculation and speculation leads to massive loss of wealth when the cycle inevitably turns against you.

In the real estate investment business, portfolio strength begins with the first property, or door. To a strategic investor, that means buying the right property the first time—and then buying another right property after that. And it's not like you're working alone, since the 10 fundamentals provide the information you need to find properties that fit your investment system.

To see how all of this works, let's look at an example. Say you want to buy a revenue property to hold for five years. Sophisticated investors know this property must cover all of its own expenses, including the mortgage and any other money borrowed to buy the property. After that, the property must yield extra cash every month over and above the operations. We call this positive cash flow. To find a property that fits this part of their system, these investors can use tools like REIN's Goldmine Score Card to make sure they are looking in a geographic area that supports their business plan: to make money. Once they find an area that has the right economic fundamentals to attract people who will want to rent places to live, these same investors can study specific properties using additional tools like the REIN Property Analyzer Form and Property Due Diligence Checklist. With this approach, they can dismiss properties that don't even remotely have a chance of weathering market storms. Each step they skip in the pre-purchase work is the equivalent of throwing life jackets overboard, leaving them dangerously exposed when the waves begin to rock the boat. Strategic investors know that it's their business to fall in love with numbers, not a piece of real estate.

## A Word about Cash Flow: Rationalizations Make You Broke

Let's be honest: newcomers to this industry often discount the ability to find positive cash flow properties in their target market. They hear about the importance of cash flow, but don't have the patience to wait for the property that will produce it. That's a huge problem the strategic investor doesn't have.

---

**The strategic investor knows that if he can't find positive cash flow properties in his target market, the system is working—not broken!**

---

The system's number one job is to help you find the right property and to protect you from rationalizing your way into the wrong property. As humans, we can find many ways to justify just about anything in our lives. In fact, we are incredibly talented at making something we want to happen seem more attractive than it really is. This propensity becomes especially dangerous when we're investing.

That's why it is quite frustrating when you hear beginning investors (and some veterans) change their investing rules because they are finding it more difficult to find properties that fit the system. Instead of hearing them proclaim that the system works when it prevents them from jumping into properties that aren't seaworthy on calm seas let alone stormy waters, these investors are throwing life jackets overboard. Why would you *assume* a property will make money every month when you can conduct the pre-property purchase due diligence to calculate cash flow and make sure it happens?

Sophisticated investors take a more prudent approach, with most of us even building in extra emergency budget expenses when calculating potential cash flow. Call me cautious but I want at least one life jacket for everyone on board *and* life boats to take us to safety, just in case.

## A Strategic Approach to Market Value

Market values are another area where non-strategic investors confuse reality with what they think they can justify. Strategically speaking, the actual price of the property only matters as a part of the cash flow equation. A million-dollar property in one region might create less cash flow than a $300,000 property in another. So if you ask me what a property is *worth*, I will tell you it's worth what the market will pay for it. Nothing less. But certainly nothing more. (While I love what market appreciation does for my business, I don't bank on it because it is not income. It is the dessert that comes at the end of the meal—right after you've eaten all of the things that actually keep you alive.)

When I tell people that my portfolio follows three principles—cash flow is king, appreciation is a bonus and every property deal must be a win-win for me, my partners and the people we're dealing with—some investors become quite confused. In their minds, these principles seem to defy conventional wisdom. My response is that long-term positive cash flow doesn't make for an exciting TV show: that's why the flip shows are so entertaining for viewers. Where the sophisticated investor looks for market intelligence and a how-to plan to follow, the emotional investor lets fear and greed cloud his judgment.

That's why I am so careful to temper enthusiasm for this business with talk of hard work. Real estate investment is not difficult. But success in this business is about future wealth and that requires that we build a sturdy, storm-proof portfolio. That takes hard work, but since it's the kind of hard work that my family's and my financial freedom depend on, I'd say it's well worth the effort.

If market newcomers are serious about making money in real estate investment, I challenge them to support their enthusiasm with education about what it takes to buy one "right" property after another. Following a system that already works definitely reduces the amount of hard work it takes to be successful.

## Use Information to Reduce Risk

When I bought my first investment property, I was acting with a friend and roommate. The next couple of houses I bought were all homes I lived in and there was never a shortage of quality advice about how that process worked. Connie and I did some first-hand research into the neighbourhoods where we might want to live. We also chose to surround ourselves with people who knew more than we did in real estate and were lucky to have a patient and knowledgeable realtor on our side.

While our real estate resources were more limited in the 1990s, we did our homework as best we could. Then, as now, quality advice helps manage the stress of buying and closing on a property. But let me be clear about what this means for real estate investors, especially if you are new to the business. First and foremost, I believe that sound investment advice, given by someone who is actually experienced and doesn't profit if you buy a property, is available; just be careful of pretenders. With that in mind, experience has taught me to take advice only from someone who meets the following three criteria:

1. They must be actively investing in real estate.
2. They must have at least 10 years of personal experience investing in real estate (which ensures they have come through the ups and downs).
3. They must have been successful over that time. This point is critical because lots of unsuccessful investors turn to teaching rather than becoming better investors.

Each of these criteria helps new investors deal with their fear of making mistakes. Like everything in life, you can rest assured we all make mistakes. Your job is to mitigate the downside of the mistakes, learn from them and, most importantly, not repeat them.

————————————— ∾ —————————————

**You can accelerate your progress on the learning curve by surrounding yourself with people who are willing to share information about the mistakes they made and who tell you how to avoid those mistakes now.**

## Just the Facts

Most, if not all of the mistakes you could possibly make have already have been made by others. That's right. Long-term investors will have made costly mistakes, such as overestimating potential cash flow and underestimating repair costs. They will have lost out on tax reductions because they have misplaced valuable receipts. They will have hired contractors who walked away from incomplete jobs or who expected pay for sub-par work. They will have first-hand experience with the financial and emotional pain that comes from working with the wrong partners. Some of them will have made these mistakes and corrected them quickly. Others will get back on track only after they lose a little more money while *justifying* their errors.

> The good news is that once you gain their trust, those who stick with strategic investing will gladly share their experiences and tell you how to fix similar problems. Sophisticated investors who haven't made specific mistakes themselves will also tell you they avoided trouble spots by knowing others who had run into them head-first!

## Warning: Lemons Will Suck You Dry

Yes, there have been times when I walked away from a property and later realized, with the benefit of 20/20 hindsight, that it would have been a good addition to my portfolio. But if the analysis at the time said no, so did I. There have also been a very small number of properties I bought that I should have rejected.

In both instances, the main reason I might have changed my mind about these properties is that the rules of the game changed after the analysis was complete and a decision made. City governments sometimes do change their collective minds, leading to situations in which long-promised infrastructure projects are suddenly either back on track or cancelled, and anticipated zoning changes either are or are not approved. These actions literally change the fundamentals and so make research that was done earlier irrelevant.

Similarly, there have been times when major employers take actions, good or bad, affecting local employment numbers after I've walked away from a property or closed a deal. My analysis simply isn't privy to all the many different variables that can come in to play.

Over time, I've learned to give myself a pat on the back every time I walk away from a property that would have weakened my portfolio because that's exactly what a sophisticated investor is supposed to do. And don't talk to me about making lemonade from lemons! While that might be an interesting analogy, I have learned to appreciate avoiding lemons. It makes real estate much more boring—and much more profitable.

## Value Facts, Not Conjecture

Be aware of low unemployment rates, which are great for housing demand, but not so great if you are trying to get a contractor to do renovations in a timely manner. In fact, there have been times, in booming markets, where I just had to walk away from properties that would have been a great deal based solely on the fact that I would not be able to renovate or repair them fast enough to get them back on the rental market in a reasonable period of time. Budget also becomes a concern in booming markets as contractors working in regions with labour shortages have to charge premium contracting rates. You can mitigate these risks if you have developed a long-term relationship with a renovation expert. The higher costs and longer turnaround times won't disappear, but having these relationships can make your work a priority.

---

**Regardless of what's at the root of the problem with a property (financial or economic fundamentals, access to renovators), if my system tells me I can't fix it within my parameters, I must move on. The fundamentals may be telling me to buy, but I simply cannot justify borrowing money to invest in a property that can't provide cash flow.**

---

I must caution the reader that while this all sounds easy on paper, it's much more difficult to do in real life. Canadian investors who were bullish on expanding their portfolios through the first three quarters of 2008 were probably not wrong in terms of how they assessed the fundamentals. The problems, if and when they arose, were often related to the *properties* they were buying, not the *economy* in which they were buying. Until September 2008, it was easy to get caught up in the market euphoria, making cash flow a secondary consideration. That was a big mistake.

That is why education is the most valuable commodity a real estate investor can get before he or she buys property.

Much of what you will need to know can be learned by surrounding yourself with successful real estate investors who are open to helping new investors get into the business. To summarize that thought: you must surround yourself with people who are achieving more. Most of the mistakes investors might make (like overestimating cash flow or underestimating the complications of tenant relations) are mistakes others have already made. The people you choose to listen to do not have to have made these mistakes themselves. But they know others who have made them. They know how to fix the mistake and will definitely understand that education is the best way to avoid problems in the first place.

Working with successful real estate investors should also help to protect your business from the vagaries of the hot tip. Investing based on inside information or hot tips will often be the opposite of what market fundamentals are saying. Even when tips prove to be right, the sophisticated investor will want to base investment decisions on his or her own examination of the data. The fact that a property may yield cash flow (and even rapidly appreciate) *if* a particular development goes ahead (like a new transportation route or construction of a major source of employment) is little consolation to an investor who buys based on a hot tip that doesn't come true. You might as well go to Vegas, put your money on red and wait for the wheel to spin. That's no way to invest, that's just pure speculation. A strategic investor would wait until the projects start, then buy from the speculators who want to get out with their quick buck. Because the investor's decision is based on the fundamentals, she gets the benefit of lower risk—with long-term profits.

In sum, the sophisticated investor may keep an eye on properties affected by a hot tip. But they're unlikely to buy until the development proceeds. Veteran investors sometimes joke that they make their money as settlers, not as pioneers.

## Beware of the Big Talker

Do take note of the fact that my advisor criteria stipulate that you get advice from experienced and *successful* real estate investors. The ugly truth about the world of real estate investing is that not every investor makes money buying, holding and selling real estate. Some advisors make money solely by giving advice, advice that is often packaged alongside strategies to market specific properties. Let me be clear: if an insider's advice is based on me buying property from him or her, I'm out.

By the same token, my business depends on my reputation as a real estate investment researcher and analyst as well as being an active investor. In other words, I eat my own cooking.

It's worth adding a note about the negative big talker: these individuals like to give advice about why you should *not* invest in real estate. Their advice is laden with stories about their own problems, or with anecdotes about problems others have had. Again, real estate investing is not something everyone can do well. But if you wouldn't take cooking lessons from someone who boils the potato pot dry, why would you take advice from a landlord who cannot keep his rental suites full or his ledger in the black?

―――――――――――― ∾ ――――――――――――

**Quality advice acknowledges that mistakes can be avoided or fixed. Those who say otherwise are not taking a sophisticated approach to real estate investment.**

## Just the Facts

Industry outsiders sometimes dismiss this notion that it is possible for successful real estate investors to be focused on a system. They are wrong. Experience tells me that real estate investors will fine-tune their system as they go. But because they deliberately seek advice from other successful investors, they never have to start from scratch in terms of figuring out what they need to do to keep their business on track.

A system does not mean there is only one way to do something. It does mean that you have to decide what works for you and then not deviate from that. Will unforeseen problems arise? Probably. And when they

do, the savvy investor goes back to his system to solve
the problem quickly and proactively. The word "system"
can be looked at as an acronym:

**S**ave
**Y**our
**S**elf
**T**ime
**E**nergy
**M**oney

## Managing for Profit

Once the right property is in his portfolio, the strategic
investor strengthens that investment by managing the property for profitability. In simplest terms, managing for profit
is all about being proactive in all aspects of the business.
From a more strategic viewpoint, keen attention to the
profitability of each new property—and making sure it is
going to be easily and properly managed—must be part of
the decision-making process. Great deals with poor management quickly become bad deals.

Managing for profit requires that investors understand
all aspects of their business, from overall property and tenant management to marketing strategies and portfolio-
management systems that are designed to help investors

deal with everything from paperwork to repairs. Each of these areas represents a profit centre for your business—a profit centre that can lose money if it's not well managed. Each of these areas also links solidly back to quality and up-to-date bookkeeping, since that's what gives you the numbers you need to make good decisions. If you are behind in your bookkeeping, you can never make a proper, non-emotional decision about a property.

The implications of not managing for profit range from the nickel-and-dime frustration of paying higher-than-necessary water bills caused by leaky toilets or dripping taps, to the higher-stakes hassles caused when vacant units throw off cash flow or force a cash infusion. Just because you have hired a property management company doesn't mean you abdicate your responsibility—you must manage the managers.

## A View from the Trenches

The global economic collapse of 2008 did not spare Canada and real estate investors were among the businesses that took a direct hit because it became more difficult to get the revenues they wanted. It was sad to observe how some investors, experiencing their first-ever downturn, decided to ignore the issues. Rather than be proactive and get more hands-on in their business, they just threw their hands in the air and gave up. These fair-weather types of investors are not strategic. They are positioned to lose money because they think results are out of their control. When the market is hot, they feel hot and on top of the world. When the market slows down, they feel helpless.

It is important to note that some Canadian investors who suddenly saw their property values suffer a rapid decline beginning in the fall and winter of 2008 had stopped investing with sophistication some time earlier, or had jumped into the market with insufficient preparation. Needless to say, their portfolios were not designed to survive significant market changes.

The biggest lesson that this downturn taught so many people is the importance of cash flow and having a cash reserve (just like every other business). Those who had quality renters, a quality property and got proactive during the downturn survived and actually grew their portfolio. They grew it by buying from those who didn't have a plan, those who never stocked their business with the life jackets and reserves that are critical to prospering throughout the entire real estate cycle. The only way these investors win is through market value increases. So when declines set in, they have no idea what to do.

Let's look at this speculator group more closely. Just because they had bought properties located in economically strong communities, these investors believed

(*continued*)

that long-term market appreciation would make their investments profitable. Some didn't even calculate cash flow. It was quite an unrealistic view, but I do understand that it's easy to get caught up in this perspective, especially if you're a beginner who has never experienced a significant economic downturn. What these investors did not know, but could have found out had they first invested in some sound market education, is that market values always rise and fall. Many investors, who at least had a modicum of understanding about markets, willfully chose to ignore this. Instead of investing with a proven system that gives investors specific tools to mitigate risk, they threw caution to the wind. Motivated by greed, many turned their backs on the cardinal principle regarding the importance of cash flow. Acting like speculators instead of sophisticated investors, they didn't mitigate risk—they ignored it.

I am pleased to tell you that many Canadian investors experienced the downturn differently. Yes, it was tough riding out the economic storm. Like the first-rate captain of a ship in a tempest, they gave 100 per cent of their attention to navigating the waves, taking an all-hands-on-deck! approach to their business.

These strategic investors immediately began regular interactions with their property management companies. Even though these companies had been hired to manage with an approach that left nothing to chance, these investors saw that different times called for different strategies. They reviewed their portfolios with care. They cut operating costs and increased marketing efforts. They kept an eye out for other ships that were in trouble, and some that had been cut adrift thanks to less-strategic captains who let the storm do its damage before shrugging and saying "it wasn't my fault." Because of their hands-on approach and strategic awareness, the strategic investors were able to strengthen their portfolios. Some even added properties on the cheap. The culmination of this experience was conclusive: proactive investing is the only way to go.

I share this because the lessons learned since 2008 have been taught by the market before and will be taught again in the next downturn. These are not lessons any investor needs to learn first-hand. Investors can be prepared or blindly sail the dark seas. Choose now.

## The Midas Trap

I speak a lot about strategic or sophisticated investors versus beginner investors. It is important to understand one very important fact: sometimes, and it's more often than I'd like to see, veteran investors begin to believe they are infallible and can do no wrong. This approach is not strategic.

What happens is that after a few wins, with very few mistakes or losses, a veteran investor may get a little lax about applying his system, undertaking his analysis and making his property choices. In fact, as strange as this seems, some actually go out and find or create mistakes so they have something to solve. Buoyed by their ability to make several good choices—or by the fact that they enjoyed some plain old-fashioned (and terribly non-strategic) good luck—these investors forget how those choices were made (cautiously and with much supporting data). They start to think their success says more about them than their system. Well, King Midas and his ability to turn everything he touched to gold was a myth—and so is the idea that some investors can buy and sell property with impunity, always making money and never making mistakes.

Motivated by their own Midas complex, which fosters greed and a belief in fast cash, these individuals buy the wrong properties because they think they can make any property profitable. Please don't fall into this trap.

The best way to avoid the Midas mistake is to stick with your system. Just because you are good at buying existing properties and making them yield positive cash flow does not mean that you are automatically going to be great at developing properties or at a different system, such as lease-to-own or flipping for profit.

## Just the Facts

Media coverage of the Canadian real estate cycle is confusing. Two experts say one thing, three others say another. For a deeper understanding of how market fundamentals impact real estate markets, pick up a copy of my book (with Kieran Trass, Greg Head and Christine Ruptash), *Secrets of the Canadian Real Estate Cycle: An Investor's Guide*. It shows investors how to make buy, hold and sell decisions based on key market indicators and uses contemporary data from the 2008 recession to illustrate how this works.

## Breaking the Law

Investors who are determined to capitalize on the peaks and valleys of the market will always be disappointed. But while there's no surefire way to know when a market is nearing the top or bottom of its cycle, the economic storms caused by illegal actions are entirely preventable. They can also derail an otherwise healthy portfolio, and that's why strategic investors will tell you that they always work within the law.

They do not sign any papers that are not accurate, nor do they misrepresent themselves in meetings with other people. While some dishonest mortgage brokers or other shady professionals may tell you it is okay to misrepresent certain facts, you must be aware that any document you sign or declaration you make represents only *you*. If an error is caught, you are the only one who pays the price. The advisor gets away scot-free, leaving you to twist in the wind. That is why it is easy for them to give bad advice.

According to the law, the rulings always go back to *intention*. As in: what was the intention of the buyer or seller for this property? If it's easy to prove that you were not going to move into a property and make it your principal residence, it is illegal to sign papers that say you do plan to move in. Signing those papers may help you get a better mortgage or to get it more easily, but it's mortgage fraud, and lawbreakers can and do go to jail for fraud.

---

**Even when it's not illegal, dishonesty is a poor foundation for a healthy portfolio.**

---

You will lose the loan when a lender or mortgage broker learns that you cannot supply the financial evidence they need to approve your mortgage. You will lose your real estate agent's trust when you tie him or her up with a sale you do not (or cannot) close.

And what do you think happens when investors try dishonest strategies more than once? You may think you are learning on the job. Others might think you are taking advantage of their expertise—and wasting their valuable time. To do their jobs well, real estate investors need to have a good working relationship with lenders, mortgage brokers, real estate agents, contractors, lawyers, accountants, property managers, tenants and other investors. The next chapter looks at how one builds a real estate investment team.

## Pocket Gold

Once a community or neighbourhood with the desired economic fundamentals is identified, sophisticated investors zero in on finding the right property. The REIN Property Analyzer Form helps them do that and I've included it here so readers can get familiar with this tool.

Investors sometimes tell me the analyzer frustrates them because it dismisses more properties that it approves. My response is pretty simple: that's the point! Buying the right property takes some work and persistence. Buying the wrong property is much easier—until you try to fix the mistake, which is much more difficult and costly than taking the time it always takes to find that right property. Let the system take care of you, so the properties you add to your portfolio take care of your financial dreams and goals.

# REIN PROPERTY ANALYZER FORM

## Property Data:

Address: _____ City/Area: _____ Date Viewed: _____

Asking Price $ _____ Size (sq ft): _____ Age: _____

Major Repairs: _____ Est Repair Cost $_____

Owner: _____ Tel: _____ Fax: _____

Source: _____ Tel: _____ Fax: _____

Overall Condition: 1  2  3  4  5

## Income & Inspection

| Suite # or Desc | # of Bedrooms | Current Rent | Projected Rent | Increase Date | Inspection Comments |
|---|---|---|---|---|---|
|  |  |  |  |  |  |
|  |  |  |  |  |  |
|  |  |  |  |  |  |
|  |  |  |  |  |  |
|  |  |  |  |  |  |

Total Monthly Rent     $_____   $_____

Total Annual Rent      $_____   $_____

## Expenses:

| | Current Annual | Current Monthly | Projected Monthly | Comments |
|---|---|---|---|---|
| Heat (gas, oil, elect, hot water, other _____) |  |  |  | Paid by Tenant / Landlord |
| Electricity |  |  |  | Paid by Tenant / Landlord |
| Water/Sewer |  |  |  | Paid by Tenant / Landlord / Condo |
| Taxes |  |  |  | Included in Mortgage Payment? |
| Condo Fee |  |  |  | Last Increase date: |
| Insurance |  |  |  | |
| Property Management | % |  |  | Current Management Rating 1 2 3 4 5 |
| Vacancy Allowance | % |  |  | Current Vacancy _____% |
| Rental Pool Mgmt | % |  |  | |
| Repairs & Maintenance | % |  |  | Overall Condition 1 2 3 4 5 |
| Resident Manager |  |  |  | Current On-site Impression 1 2 3 4 5 |
| Other: |  |  |  | |

TOTAL MONTHLY        $_____   $_____

TOTAL MONTHLY INCOME less TOTAL MONTHLY EXPENSES (Before Debt Service)=

Current: $ _____        Projected: $ _____

**TOTAL PROJECTED INCOME  $_____**

## Mortgaging/Debt Service:

| | Balance | Interest Rate | Expiry Date | Monthly Payment | |
|---|---|---|---|---|---|
| 1st Mortgage | | % | | | P I T |
| 2nd Mortgage | | % | | | F I T |
| Vendor Take Back | | % | | | F I T |
| Other | | % | | | P I T |

**TOTAL DEBT SERVICE** $ _____

**NET CASH FLOW** $ _____

## Purchase Details:

PROJECTED PURCHASE PRICE $ _____

| | |
|---|---|
| 1st Mortgage Funding | ($ _____) |
| 2nd Mortgage Funding | ($ _____) |
| Vendor Take Back | ($ _____) |
| Other Funding | ($ _____) |

TOTAL DEBT FUNDING ($ _____)
**DOWN PAYMENT REQUIRED** $ _____

## Purchase Costs:

| | |
|---|---|
| Professional Inspection | $ _____ |
| Value Appraisal | $ _____ |
| Real Property Report (Survey) | $ _____ |
| Mortgage Set-Up Costs | $ _____ |
| Mortgage Broker Fees | $ _____ |
| Legal Costs (incl disbursements) | $ _____ |
| Staying Power Fund | $ _____ |
| Immediate Repairs | $ _____ |
| Immediate Renovations | $ _____ |
| Other _____ | $ _____ |
| Other _____ | $ _____ |

**TOTAL PURCHASE COSTS** $ _____

**TOTAL CASH REQUIRED TO CLOSE** (Down payment + Purchase costs) $ _____

1. Does this property take me closer to my goal or farther away? ❑ Closer ❑ Farther
2. Does this property fit my system? ❑ Yes ❑ No
3. Will this property be impeccably property managed? ❑ Yes ❑ No
4. Who will manage the property? _____

# Chapter Four

# Building the Team

How MANY TIMES have we heard that success in real estate is all about "location, location, location"?

Too many times to count. But if I was asked to name the one thing that tipped my own real estate portfolio in the direction of success, I'd probably start humming that old Beatles tune about getting by with a little help from my friends. That's right, my thoughts would rarely turn to the specifics of where these properties are located. Location matters—but from where I sit, relationships matter a whole lot more.

Whenever I speak about real estate investing being built on teamwork, I get a lot of strange looks from the audience. Why? Simply because the majority of new investors believes that real estate is a lone-wolf endeavour. When investors first start out they believe they have to do it all themselves and even when they interact with others, they do it with the attitude that these helpers (realtors, inspectors, etc.) are a dime a dozen. This habit of underestimating the value of their teammates will become the brick wall that stops them on their long-term journey.

Sophisticated real estate investors see things differently, probably because each of them has a trunkful of examples demonstrating how teammates have added great value to their investment businesses or kept them out of hot water. They probably know a real estate agent whose knowledge of city planning or coming bylaw changes allowed them to take advantage of the changes. Or they know an astute contractor who identified hidden building problems and solved them before they became financial disasters. Others will have profited from the legal advice given by an experienced real estate lawyers whose expertise translated into a trouble-free joint venture agreement, or from an accountant who structured their deals to save a tremendous amount of tax. Sophisticated investors understand the importance of building a team and treat its members as an important part of their long-term game plan.

## "Put me in, Coach!"

Real estate investors are often described as being the captains of their teams but that doesn't quite describe their role. Successful investors are, in reality, the coaches, general managers and presidents of their own home teams. To create long-term success, the investor must choose the players they want to have on their team, and when they need to trade, fire or mentor them. The investor makes the final decisions. Like successful coaches, investors do not have to put the puck in the net—but they do need to surround themselves with people who can. They build their teams with people who are experts in their field, empower them to use this expertise and do not expect them to be great at all aspects of real estate. They would never put a renovation contractor in charge of finding mortgages, nor would they ask the mortgage broker to renovate a basement suite.

The team is built by proactively managing its members and how they work together. The coach–GM–president changes personnel when needed and makes it his or her business to provide a productive working atmosphere so the players want to stay and contribute. This big-picture approach allows the real estate investor to pack his bench with a specialized team of experts, several of whom may need to play the captain's role for the time it takes to accomplish a specific task. The investor won't need to call on every player every day, but he knows that every player must be ready to do his or her job when called upon.

---

**Investors, in other words, must be *intentional* and *strategic* about how they network to keep and improve their teams.**

---

Coaches respect team members and do not play them against each other. They also are not shy about the fact that a team can benefit from new ideas, a point of view that helps the coach keep an eye out for innovation and new talent.

If you're new to investing and unsure about who you need on your team, I encourage you to make it your first order of business to find out. These people comprise the foundation of your investment system and when they apply their expertise to your business, everyone wins.

## The Real Estate Investment Team

Take your player search up a notch by looking for people who are real estate investors as well as specialists in their individual fields. When you make that criterion part of your filter, the expertise you rely on will come from real-life experience, not just theory. Here are some of the main players you'll need on your bench. For a more detailed look at their importance, read my book, *Real Estate Investing in Canada 2.0: Creating Wealth with the ACRE System.*

- Real estate agents
- Mortgage brokers and bankers
- Property managers
- Inspectors, appraisers
- Bookkeeper
- Professional advisors (lawyers, accountants)
- Other successful investors
- Joint-venture partners
- Life partners

## The Role of Mutual Respect

The problem with using a sports analogy to help people understand real estate investment is that professional athletes have signed contracts that outline what they can and cannot be asked to do. Real estate investors rarely have actual contracts with their players. This means loyalty must be earned (not bought and paid for) and this is why mutually-beneficial relationships play such a pivotal role in an investor's long-term success.

Too many real estate investment gurus give short shrift to the importance of relationships. They encourage investors to see themselves as the captains of ships sailing in waters inhabited only by captains of other real estate investment ships. In their scenario, these captains might work together for a short and mutually-beneficial period of time, but mostly they will compete against one another. In this short-term thinking scenario, success comes from access to insider information and hot tips that must be acted upon within a limited time frame. Because information yields competitive advantages, the captains of these ships often work alone. That approach creates too much unnecessary stress.

Yes, real estate investment is competitive. Even so, there is ample room for cooperation and investors who miss this point will probably miss a whole lot of business opportunities!

## How to Listen to Your Team Members

The need to listen to your team members is fundamental to this notion of mutual cooperation and respect. Indeed, the ability to listen to others is one of the most important skills a real estate investor brings to his or her business. That logic is twofold. First, if you've done a good job of getting the right person into your meeting, you will be listening to someone who has trusted expertise to share. You do not need to be a property management expert in order to learn about property management from an expert. Secondly, the more you show you are a listener, the more frequently those on your team will listen to you. This takes the conversations to whole new levels.

Newcomers to real estate investment often leave networking meetings with a fistful of business cards and several promises of future breakfast and lunch dates—they go for quantity, not quality connections. These individuals may be excited by a conversation with a potential team member, perhaps a mortgage broker, who has the experience and strategies that would have a direct and positive impact on the investor's business. Instead of pursuing this one important lead, the greenhorn may think she has to set up future meetings with several of the people she met. She may even mistakenly believe that she doesn't need to meet the mortgage broker until she needs a mortgage. So rather than build an important relationship, she takes that individual for granted and treats him like any other person she's met.

By not taking the time to meet with and listen to the mortgage broker, this investor misses an opportunity to establish what could be a truly beneficial long-term relationship. Sure, there are some advantages to meeting a lot of people very fast, but if that's your standard operating practice, you may end up knowing a lot of people—but have trusted relationships with very few. Yes, it is important to attend networking meetings where you try to soak up a whole bunch of information that's not useful to you today, but which may be helpful tomorrow. What you really need, however, is to set a goal of meeting one single person at these meetings and really getting to know them. Hear their story, discover what they have to offer, and do a lot more listening than talking. In other words, change your measure of success from the number to the depth of your contacts. By doing so, you can choose the right team players and you will be introduced to people whom they know, leading to other quality potential team members. Speed is not the answer—strength is. That's right. People who know people also get to know *other* people.

—————————— ∾ ——————————

**Sophisticated real estate investors value their quality connections because they lead to other quality connections!**

—————————————————————————

# You Make Money Buying Quality Properties, Not by Unplugging Toilets!

Another greenhorn mistake is made by the new real estate investor who refuses to bring on new team members because she thinks she really has to do all the work herself. Here, the investor's short-term focus on saving pennies stifles long-term business development, something successful real estate entrepreneurs recognize as "stepping over dollars to get to dimes." Instead of taking their time to review new and potential properties presented by the realtor on their team, they are too busy unplugging toilets or sorting through receipts—jobs the sophisticated investors would hire out to a property manager and bookkeeper.

The bottom line is that deep and meaningful business relationships occur only when relationships are mutually beneficial. They arise from situations where the members of that relationship share a mutual dependence that will benefit from their cooperation. For example, a contractor who performs quality work at affordable prices will help an investor to get her property onto the rental market, freeing both for their next joint endeavour. Similarly, a good real estate agent will help that investor find more quality property for her portfolio. Win-win.

Once an investor understands that his relationship with his team members has to be a two-way street, he will see that it is inappropriate to measure network strength in terms of its size (or the number of business cards collected). Quality trumps quantity every time.

## A View from the Trenches

There have been four times in my investment career when I brought the wrong person onto my team and paid a price. Despite being very careful with my due diligence and feeling, at least initially, that I had the right individual in place, I later discovered that I was wrong.

Being something of a rescuer by nature, my first instinct was to fix the problem by fixing the individual with whom I was having difficulties. Convinced that I could bring these people up to the standard I expected, I invested additional time, effort and money in these relationships and tried to make things work.

Hindsight is a great teacher and I now follow what I call a "slow to hire, quick to fire" philosophy. In other words, I do my due diligence before bringing new members on board. And then, if things do not work out and there is no quick solution, I end the business relationship. It's not working out for you. It's not working out for me. Let's move on.

I'll be the first to admit that this approach can seem harsh. Truth be known, I want people on my team who want to play at the top level of their profession so that they can profit accordingly. In the early days of my real estate investment career, I thought I could fix business relationships that weren't working. Experience taught me that dragging people kicking and screaming to success is exhausting. It also limits your own success and that will negatively impact other relationships, both business and personal.

Experience has also taught me to sharpen the saw before it's needed to cut wood. In terms of my relationships, this means I am always on the lookout for potential additions to my team. I interview property managers before I need them. I explore costs and working relationships with contractors before I have even identified a property that needs renovations or repairs. I listen to real estate agents who have particular knowledge of a potential geographic region even if I haven't yet bought a property there. I ask other investors about their property appraisers and inspectors. These conversations give me the kind of information that I can literally bank on in the future.

## Practise Active Listening

Active listening takes practice. To make active listening part of your intentional and strategic business practice, try these suggestions from professional communicators:

1. **Focus.** Active listeners face the people they're talking to and maintain eye contact.
2. **Consider the setting.** The networking meeting or seminar environment can get in the way of a good

conversation. If you want to get to know a particular person better, ask for a follow-up meeting in a place with fewer distractions.

3. **Be honest.** Be forthright about why you'd like to get to know the person better.

   - "I've heard you may be interested in a joint venture? Can we talk?"
   - "I like what you said about tenant relationships. I've had a few problems with this. Could we get together to talk about how you filter tenants?"
   - "I'm interested in joint-venture partnerships but don't know how to find money partners. Could we have coffee and talk about how you deal with these issues?"

4. **Ask open-ended questions.** If you want information, go after it. Ask questions such as: "What did you do next?" or "Why do you think that strategy worked?" Go for detail, but be incredibly respectful of the person's time and expertise. Many people who are experts get inundated with requests for information. If you want to build a relationship with someone, stand out by finding ways to help them as well!

5. **Avoid conversation clutter.** If you need help with a certain problem, fine. But don't ask someone else's opinion and then talk about why you would do something different. Are you *listening* to them—or

trying to get them to listen to you? Figure that out before you take up someone's time.

6. **Keep your mouth shut.** Smart business people learn more by listening to others than by hearing themselves talk. You can't learn with your mouth open! Practise keeping your mouth shut, even when you do not like what you're hearing. Also avoid giving a quick response to information, especially if it is information that's made you unhappy. The fast answer is likely to be more emotional than rational. Remember you asked for their advice, counsel or opinion—and that is what you are getting. This is not an opportunity to argue. Take the information, use what you can and dispose of the rest. Investors can teach other members of their team to practise this approach by modelling it first!

## How to Get Your Team to Listen to You

If you weren't convinced before, the reasons you need to listen to team members should now be obvious. They are on your team because you think they have something to offer your business. Even though you have different goals, the relationship is reciprocal because it helps all of you meet those goals. Team members won't necessarily gain a direct share in your wealth, but your success in real estate investment should have a positive impact on their own business or employment situation. Besides all that, the reason you need to listen to them is that you want them to listen to *you*.

I know an investor who was frustrated because he thought some members of his team were deliberately wasting his time. His real estate agent called with news of several supposedly great properties. Unfortunately, all four completely missed the mark and the investor lost an entire day to the process of checking them out. One was priced significantly under market value but needed a lot of work— work that would cost more time and money than that investor's system allowed. Two others were located in neighbourhoods adjacent to a road that was destined for expansion. Homeowners were already embroiled in a fight with city hall over expropriation, but listing prices did not reflect the uncertainty. When they pulled up to the second property with the same problem, the investor didn't even want to get out of the car. The last house he was shown was located in a highly sought-after neighbourhood. It was almost certain to lead to a bidding war.

I sympathized with the investor, but encouraged him to evaluate the situation. If this real estate agent has done a good job to date, call a meeting to express your concern that he seems to have lost touch with what your business is about (short-term cash flow, long-term appreciation). Try to ascertain his understanding of the local rental market. Is it out of touch with what you see—or is he trying to get you to think outside of the box? If it's the latter, find out why he thought these properties would work for your business. If he's been with you for some time, maybe he doesn't understand that your system has evolved to focus on very specific kinds of properties. This may be a good time to remind him that you don't see house-shopping as recreation. For you, it's business.

Getting property managers to listen to you is also important and you can foster communication by listening to them. What would make their job easier? What can you do to facilitate that? Why is that not possible at this time? What do you need from them? Why does that matter?

Never forget that these relationships with your team members are the foundation of your long-term business success. They can strengthen it, or wear it down. When you are frustrated by a particular team member's contribution, take some time to think about the issue before you confront him or her. Respect their time and expertise. You do not have to tell your accountant that you think he complains too much about the state of your files, or that your property manager should have anticipated a major maintenance issue if only he'd been doing his job right. But you should ask what you can do to make their jobs easier, and you can tell them that you are serious about learning how to improve the way you conduct your business, so that it improves the way they conduct their business. In sum, learn and listen and then act accordingly.

## Growing Your Team

Getting others to listen to you implies the need to listen to them first. This builds trust, and trust engenders loyalty. But loyalty to particular team members should never stop you from scouting free agents. This is especially pertinent when it comes to property management, realtors and mortgage brokers. These are critical players and a good team GM builds a farm team so she doesn't get caught short if one of her key team players stops performing.

Scouting prospective team members also gives you an advantage when the time comes to add new players when your portfolio changes or expands. For example, a lot of investors launch their portfolios by taking care of property management themselves. Once they own several properties, especially if those properties are not located near where they live and work, they start looking for professional managers. Sophisticated real estate investors will advise the beginner to get a quality property manager on their team early on. Yes, it costs money, but it's important to keep an eye on the big picture. Instead of handling the nitty-gritty of replacing furnace filters or vetting prospective renters, these investors can focus their attention on adding quality properties to their portfolio and analyzing their existing portfolio to make sure they still fit their business model and exit strategy.

Over time, sophisticated investors also find that their team changes as their business changes. Investors who transition from single to multi-family housing or those who expand their buy-and-hold portfolios to include fixing up properties for the resale market, or buying properties for the lease-to-own market, will probably find themselves working with different team members. Different experts often have access to different team players precisely because their portfolios require specialized knowledge.

Investors must also be cognizant of the fact that they work in the real world. Real estate agents, contractors, property managers and professional advisors come and go. Mortgage brokers retire. Bank employees take transfers. Be prepared to deal with change!

---

**Never think your team is so perfect it can never change. That kind of complacency leaves a portfolio unnecessarily exposed to the career changes of its supporting cast!**

---

## Set a Gold Standard for Ethical Conduct

I have met real estate investors who seem confused about what constitutes ethical behaviour. If that's your starting point, then I urge you to consider legal boundaries as your line in the sand. Investors who break the law should be prepared to pay the consequences. In 2010, one of Canada's largest banks sued hundreds of Albertans for mortgage fraud. By the time that case came to light, Ontario had already increased its penalties for mortgage fraud.

Mortgage fraud is complicated. At its most basic level, it involves individuals signing false mortgage documents. If anyone ever asks you to sign a document that is not true (like one that says you plan to live in a property even though you do not plan to make it your residence), walk away from the deal—and fire that team member. These types of players are poison to your team. If you want long-term success, you need to distance yourself from unethical people as fast you can.

Most of the ethical issues real estate investors will confront have less to do with breaking the law than with breaking the mutual-respect component of the relationships that keep their businesses on track. Just because something is not illegal does not make it okay. REIN members actually follow a defined code of ethics that calls on them to be sure they conduct their business in an ethical and legal manner. As part of that code, they agree to ensure "that others, within the group as well as outside the group, are treated ethically and with respect by members." This code sets REIN apart. The real estate community in Canada is really not that large and your reputation as an investor is paramount to your success.

Real estate is not about taking advantage of vulnerable vendors. Nor is it about fooling the banks by not revealing every fact. It's definitely not about setting up your team members to fail. Real estate investing is a business and the community has a long, long memory. If you screw someone over, expect people to hear about it. Doors suddenly will be closed to you and you will never be told why.

## Stand by Your Word

REIN's approach to ethical issues is radically different from some in the industry. I would argue that it outlines a strategy that's best suited for those who want to be seen as sophisticated investors. As its starting point, REIN expects those who enter agreements to do so with the intention of living by the terms of that agreement. This does not mean that situations never change. It does mean that various team members give each other the information they need to try and enact agreements that can withstand the tests of time and changing circumstances. The REIN code expects that participants will reveal all relevant aspects of the transaction to the respective parties, including real estate agents, bankers, buyers and partners. Further, ethical investors never ask others, including other investors, to break the law or to act unethically. They are required never to share inaccurate information, and never deliberately to omit essential information.

## Own Your Role as the Investor

The ethical approach is underlined by the fact that sophisticated investors are committed to taking responsibility for their own actions and results. Due diligence on all properties, parties and deal structures falls on the shoulders of individual investors. This is critically important.

---

**Investors who think they can blame someone else for poor decisions, or share the blame for poor decisions with others, miss the most salient point of real estate investment: the onus always comes back to the investor. You are in this business to make money— and you can't put blame in the bank!**

---

You must always take responsibility for the bad results in your business if you also want to take credit for the good results. Ignore this rule and you risk your reputation as a professional.

The short- and long-term repercussions of the U.S. mortgage fiasco serve as a useful reminder of the fact that investors must always be wary of how their actions in the investment and larger community reflect on this industry at large. Why is this business so often associated with hucksters and get-rich-quick schemes that go bad? Because too few investors stand up when they see others taking actions that damage the reputations of so many others. Make it your business to do business with people of integrity.

## The Golden Rule

Newcomers to real estate investment sometimes struggle with the particulars of what constitutes unethical practice. So let me be clear: unethical actions are actions you would not want someone else to do to you.

Some of the most common issues with ethics arise in investor dealings with real estate agents. Investors are under no legal obligation to work with a particular real estate agent. That does not mean there are no ethical consequences to your choices. One of the most ethically egregious errors made by investors is also one of the most common. It involves working with selected real estate agents and then trying to cut them out of the deal to shave a few percentage points off your final costs. Your actions are shared throughout the investment community and it engenders two big problems for investors: distrust and disloyalty. If people deal with you knowing you are not honest, they will often use that as an excuse to act dishonestly as well.

Similarly, if a mortgage broker has shopped your mortgage and put a deal on the table, it is not ethical to then take that best deal to another bank and ask them to beat it. You are in business to make money. Fair enough. That does not give you the right to take advantage of others. You may feel like you won by doing so, but those wins are short-term and can lead to long-term losses. You will never win the championship by undermining your team and losing the trust of your team members.

## From Player to Partner

Nothing underlines the value of good working relationships with your team members than the fact that good news travels fast—and bad news travels even faster. Real estate investors who want to grow their portfolios generally realize that the best way to do this is to bring in money partners. One of the first things a successful investor will tell you is that the money you need is most likely to come from the people you know. Members of your team may have money to invest, or know others who do.

There are good reasons why you may need to switch up the individual members of your team. Always work with integrity.

## Success at Home Plate

I also want to challenge real estate investors to think about the most important members of your real estate investment team: your family. These are the people who stand behind home plate and they (even if they're still in the future!) are the reason you invest in real estate.

Some investors believe it is wise to keep portfolio details, particularly problems, from their life partners. They think this is okay because they are protecting their partners from information they would not understand or do not need to know. That is a terrible idea. As the leader of your investment team, you want to bring all partners on board. I have seen some pretty creative ways to keep secrets, but secrets can almost never be sustained. The money you use to buy investment property is real: you cannot hide profits and you certainly cannot hide losses.

---

**Never compromise the integrity of your personal relationships to invest in real estate.**

---

Richard and Emma McTavish, the subjects of my first book, *Real Estate Investing in Canada 2.0: Creating Wealth with the ACRE System,* learned that the best way to deal with Emma's apprehension about real estate investment was to teach her how it worked. Because Richard kept her in the information loop, she came to understand and support what he was trying to do. Together, they mastered an investment system that balanced risk and opportunity. When faced with a business problem they couldn't answer on their own, they sought information from mentors and team members. They also learned that while real estate investment is all about passive investment, passive investment does not equal easy money. Sophisticated real estate investors make decisions that enable them to sleep at night precisely because they do not chase fast cash.

## A View from the Trenches

My wife Connie and I invest as partners and she handles a great deal of our portfolio's paperwork and all of its bookkeeping. To make our business and our marriage work, we have learned to separate the two. We set up regular meetings to talk business, but try not to let the business of real estate trickle into the rest of our relationship. Like active listening, this gets easier with practice. I can honestly say it took me about a year to get used to the fact that I needed to wait until our Thursday afternoon meetings to talk about the specifics of our business. In retrospect, this approach has become an integral part of our strategic commitment to keep emotion out of our business decisions. Without these rules, our 25-plus years of marriage would never have been as happy.

## Mutual Respect

I know investors who tried to keep business secrets from life partners and I can tell you that this doesn't ever make sense. These secrets usually involve some kind of bad news. Let me assure you that hiding information, good or bad, compromises your decision-making process. It is an emotional response to a situation that can only be repaired or mitigated through rational thought and decision-making. Besides, if you'll keep secrets in one part of your life, how can a life partner not assume you'll do it in others?

While working together has worked very well for Connie and me, it does not work for everyone. One of the most common errors I see investors make involves pushing a life partner into a direct role in the business, even if he or she lacks the talent, passion or expertise to play that role. If a partner doesn't want to keep the books or spend her nights and weekends ripping out kitchens or painting rental suites, do not make her do it. These are great examples of short-sighted and ultimately unproductive ploys meant to save money. Real estate investment is a risky business. You can make money in any market, but you can lose money too. If your life partner does not want to take an active role in managing your portfolio, don't force the issue.

By the same token, if your life partner wants to learn more about the business and wants to take a more active role, then that is something you should develop. I've seen a lot of couples come together over real estate. This is often a development that emerges over time and if your partner's interest is sincere, it is definitely worth nurturing. Consider attending real estate networking meetings together or making time for your partner to hone his or her skills in a particular aspect of the business, be it bookkeeping or property management.

## Pocket Gold

Strategic investors understand the importance of having and building a team. These teams are built one player at a time and are solidified with good rules of communications. We call them the Rules of Engagement. The rules help investors focus on building open and trusting relationships!

When communicating with team members:

1. Set goals and write them down so everyone agrees on the expected outcome.
2. Have an agenda for every meeting, and stick to it. No rambling or tangents.
3. Separate the person from the problem. Come up with solutions, not blame.
4. Discover the team member's real motivations. Often it is not money, even if they say it is.
5. Only respond to reason, not pressure. (Stick with your system!)
6. Be willing to walk away before you say something you'll regret.

7. Become a true listener because you can't learn when you are talking.
8. Be patient, clear and forthright. Sometimes it's uncomfortable, but in the end it always leads to the right conclusion.
9. Be confident when choosing team members. If you are hesitant, go with your gut instinct.
10. Never abuse the relationship or take it for granted.
11. Do what you said you'd do and expect the same from the other party.

# Chapter Five

# The Investor Mentality

SOME SOPHISTICATED real estate investors are big believers in the Law of Attraction—the idea that people can attract good and bad things into their lives by virtue of their positive and negative thoughts. Others will tell you that success comes strictly from hard work and honesty, and still others will tell you that in real estate, as in life, what goes around comes around. When I hear investors debating these ideas, I think of that song, *Funny the Way It*

*Is,* by the Dave Matthews Band. That song reminds me that life is complicated; and people have different opinions because they've had different life experiences. What all these philosophical positions have in common is the idea that if people are successful in real estate, it is because they set out to be successful.

This is what investment insiders call the "investor mentality"—and it is essential to building a successful portfolio. Strategic investors do not wander into grey areas and they certainly never break the law; they would never be associated with people who do. They maintain healthy relationships in their personal and professional lives because they value the people they've chosen to hang out with. They put little stock in good luck, but are big believers in hard work.

I've always enjoyed philosophical discussions about real estate investment because I think they help investors take a critical look at where their businesses are and whether their present focus still fits their long-term goals. A long-term perspective is important for those who want to make a plan for where they want their businesses to go. In sum, successful real estate investors run businesses that follow proven systems. They learn how to let economic fundamentals guide their business decisions and are careful to make decisions based on market information rather than emotion. They invest for long-term wealth creation and for future financial security. Does this mean real estate investment, done right, is a sure thing? Obviously not.

———————— ∼ ————————

**The goal of a strategic investor is to get out of the way of the system—and the right investor mentality is essential.**

## Success Is a Habit—Beware of the Sasquatch!

This notion of successful real estate investment as the thinking person's business is essential to what I teach. You do not need to know everything there is to know about real estate investment before you buy your first revenue property. You can, however, learn almost everything you need to know to protect your downside and increase your chances of an upside. Success is a habit—and habits begin when you decide what you will *do*.

I have often heard that investors haven't bought because they are stuck in analysis paralysis. That tells me that they are getting in the way of their chosen investment system. Strategic investors know that there is never a perfect property. Beginners without a system to guide their analysis are often stymied by the search for one perfect, risk-free, no pain opportunity. This is what I like to call the Sasquatch—because while many have heard about it, but no one has seen the beast in real life.

The really good news is that both the knowledge and the mentality required to be successful in real estate investment can be obtained. Then, once the knowledge and strategies are known, they can be practised until they become habits.

The truth is that real estate investing is a serious business, and without successful habits, you risk a lot of money, pain and potential bankruptcy. With good habits you can position yourself and your family for long-term financial success. That is why you must either do it right, or don't do it at all. As you develop your habits you also start honing your intuition for deals and the skills to close them. In other words your investor mentality begins to take shape. In the beginning you should aim to use a proven system and research, mostly gleaned from other sources, to:

1. overcome doubt about your plan of action;
2. complete due diligence on a deal that helps you balance risk and reward;
3. understand the importance of removing emotions from the decision to let the analysis of sound market data direct you;
4. focus on your *next* piece of property, rather than letting yourself be overwhelmed by the task of building a big portfolio; and
5. most importantly, practise following through.

## Overcome Self-Doubt

To be a real estate investor, one must learn how to overcome self-doubt or defeat a lack of confidence, both of which are toxic to the evolution of the investor mentality. One cannot make success a habit if you never put smart investment strategies into practice. But confidence, in and of itself, is not enough! You must have confidence not only in yourself (many people have that), but in the direction you are taking (cash flow real estate investing) and confidence in your system.

According to Peter Kinch, one of the country's leading mortgage-education professionals, confidence, credibility and integrity (CCI) are the factors that separate those who *want* to be sophisticated real estate investors from those who really *are* successful investors. Peter is the author of the bestselling book, *The Canadian Real Estate Action Plan: Proven Investment Strategies to Kick Start and Build Your Portfolio*, and he has discovered that one group *wants* while the other group *acts*.

I offer that information with one major word of warning: there is a difference between having confidence in your system and making decisions based on ego. The kind of false confidence that's based on ego has been the downfall of many an investor. As success begins to be created, some ego-boosted investors forget about the system that got them there. They start to believe that it's all about them and that they are smarter than the market. This is when portfolios begin to go off the rails. Once the ego kicks in, decisions are no longer based on the due diligence and analysis that helped create their success. Instead, decisions now follow an I-know-better thought process. Let's be frank. Real confidence is not self-delusion.

---

**Confidence has a calming influence that allows an investor to move forward with care, caution and commitment.**

---

## The Credibility Factor

The confidence component is easy to understand. Real estate investors apply their own initiative, skills and team members to every business problem they encounter, and they use that combination to build a solid investment portfolio. The actions they take today directly affect their financial security tomorrow.

Entrepreneurs obviously need a certain amount of self-assurance, and the best kind of self assurance comes from knowing what they're talking about. Credibility comes from their expertise, their experience and their track record. That is what makes individuals credible as real estate investors. Their actions are in direct contrast to the Big Talkers (who talk a lot so that they don't have to answer questions). In the end, credibility is a measurable commodity, which is directly driven by an investor's track record in real estate as well as their consistency in the following actions. Credible real estate investors:

1. show up on time for appointments;
2. do what they say they will do;
3. under-promise and over-deliver;
4. know they're judged on the reputation of the people they choose to do business with; and
5. like knowing their record can speak for itself.

## Live with Integrity

How you run your life, your business and your investments is a choice. By operating from a place of integrity, you act consistently from a foundation of honesty, empathy and respect. Integrity is a lynchpin that binds a sophisticated investor's business together. With it, the business is strong and can weather winds and storms. Without it, the business and its owner's reputation can crumble into nothing.

Your integrity is directly affected by the integrity of those around you. You can live your life with 100 per cent integrity. But if the partners, mentors, team members or friends in your life do not share that commitment to doing the right thing, people outside your circle will begin to assume that you are the same as the company you keep. That may not seem fair, but it is how the real world works.

---
~
---

**Honesty is not negotiable.**

---

In sum, credible business people who act with integrity are the kind of people who can act with confidence because they have a well-developed habit of saying what they mean and then doing what they promise. People who act with integrity gain a reputation for being credible and that reputation, combined with proven actions, leads to confidence. Remember to build your investment business on all three: confidence, credibility and integrity. Acting together you get the business equivalent of a three-legged stool. Take away one or two of those legs and you're doomed to fail.

## Fear Is Not the Enemy

So how does someone who is new to this business overcome self-doubt and a lack of confidence? What about investors who find themselves plagued by self-doubt as they encounter turbulence for the first time or are confronted with wave after wave of what appears to be very bad news about the economy?

First, understand that fear is not your enemy. Fear keeps us from stepping off ledges when blindfolded and from jumping into choppy waters when we are not wearing a life jacket. What would make those two activities okay—and maybe even fun? Information and the tools to protect your-self and reduce the risk of harm.

The same logic applies to real estate investment. Fear is solidly and deeply rooted in the unknown. You do not borrow large amounts of money without knowing how it will be paid back. Applying that logic to other aspects of the real estate investment business, you also don't hire a lawyer to write a joint-venture agreement if she's never written one before. Similarly, you don't let tenants move into a rental property before their applications are properly vetted.

Do you see where I'm going? Having a system that forces you to ask the right questions, no matter what scenario you are entering, is critical to building confidence. Even long-term, successful and strategic investors have moments of self-doubt and few people will be able to eliminate negative thoughts entirely. This is why the investor mentality, and the system that supports it, are paramount.

---

**The investor mentality will push you to remember that your decisions are system-dependent.**

---

The system helps the investor, whether she is new or experienced, to ask the right questions and get the answers she needs to hear. Instead of letting self-doubt hold them back, the investor mentality will propel them—and their portfolios—forward.

In reality, fear dissipates as proper information is gathered. Because the strategic investor is guided by a system, he knows what information to look for and where to find it. He also knows that gathering ineffective or irrelevant information bogs down the decision-making process, adds to analysis paralysis and compounds the problems caused by fear and hesitation. That's right: quality information strengthens the investor mentality and your CCI index!

## Hone that Investor Mentality!

Fear and self-doubt are normal. Sophisticated investors learn to recognize what happens to them when these emotions—or stress—cloud their decision-making process. Once they acknowledge the real problem, they deal with it. Ignoring a problem only makes it bigger. For example, if you are concerned about the media talk of housing bubbles and economic distress, review the fundamentals and make your decisions based on facts. Similarly, if you're unhappy with your property manager, make a few notes and call a meeting. Frustrated by a bad tenant? Pull out the tools you use to filter tenants to see where you went wrong and then revise your filter accordingly.

The frightened investor and the investor under stress act rashly. The strategic investor acts with authority.

## Balance Risk and Reward: The Role of Due Diligence

No amount of confidence, even when accompanied by credibility and integrity, can erase the fact that all types of investments have risks as well as potential rewards. Someone with an investor mentality recognizes those risks, analyzes them without emotion and then works to mitigate them. Unsophisticated investors get themselves in trouble by blindly (or willfully) taking actions that ignore the risks. Others err when they fail to take action because they freeze in the face of perceived risks. Strategic investors know that it is critical to complete detailed due diligence on all aspects of their business. They work through their fear because their system tells them what they need to do, and their investor mentality keeps them on track for success.

## The System

Real estate, when done correctly, can provide long-term financial results along with the occasional home-run profit that accrues from equity appreciation. Investors who manage their business without a system to guide them will find themselves chasing the short-term money while ignoring the long-term wins. With bases loaded, a walk delivers a run. Striking out while attempting to hit a grand slam delivers *nada*.

The system I use to keep those bases loaded is called the Authentic Canadian Real Estate (ACRE) system. Designed to focus on cash flow and yield, ACRE also positions investors to take advantage of any potential home-run opportunities. That has worked well for so many Canadian investors because it addresses and mitigates risks by forcing investors, rookie and veteran alike, to think before they act. Because they know what a real estate portfolio based on long-term sustainable wealth looks like, they take the specific action. These investors:

- choose a region, then a neighbourhood and then a property;
- decide who they need on their team before they hire;
- carefully vet tenants before they move in; and
- line up joint-venture partners before they have a property deal in the works.

This business-like approach teaches investors to respect risk. In baseball, a home-run king's record often features an enormous number of strikeouts, too. The same applies in real estate. If investors always focus on large potential equity appreciation, their chances of losing increase dramatically. Instead of positioning their portfolios to survive a market downturn, these non-strategic investors risk all of their future wealth by relying on a giant value increase as their only profit centre!

~

**Strategic investors love to take advantage of market appreciation—but they *bank* on cash flow.**

This sophisticated strategy views investment success as a habit, not luck. Keep hitting singles and doubles and, every once in a while, you'll pop one over the fence.

In sum, sophisticated investors follow a system that values checklists, consistent action and teamwork. This strategy respects the fact that a proven system is organic and matures along with the investor (because everyone gets better with practice). At its core, this system-based approach allows for geographic adjustments without compromising its basic structure. What works for an investor in downtown Toronto will not necessarily work for an investor in Fort McMurray or Halifax—but the fundamentals used to decide what properties to buy will never change!

## Of Death and Taxes

The sophisticated investor's focus on long-term wealth also yields tax advantages because he pays strategic attention to the taxable difference between income and capital gains. Investors who chase after the big hits (where an increase in value is the only profit potential) will find themselves unable to claim capital gains for tax purposes. This income will be taxed at the highest rate possible. Remember: people who make a profit pay taxes. But it is not how much money you make in a deal—it is how much you *keep* that matters.

Instead of riding a speculative roller coaster and surviving its peaks and valleys of profit and loss, sophisticated investors follow a sustainable system that saves them time, grief and money. They let the system do most of the work!

## Value the Due Diligence Process

Due diligence is considered useless work by many speculators, especially those swinging only for home runs. What they don't understand is that profits are always the product of the diligence process. I, too, used to think that it was my lawyer's and realtor's responsibility to make sure the property was right. Boy, was that a mistake! It cost me a bundle, not only because I was on the financial hook to fix the problem that my own due diligence should have revealed, but also because I overpaid for the property in the first place.

Those experiences taught me to value the due diligence process and helped me to develop a systematic approach. This includes a checklist that I use to this day (and have shared in the ACRE system). As outlined in earlier chapters of this book, ACRE's lasting strength lies with how it helps investors assemble the pieces of the whole. The due diligence portion is designed to force you to look carefully at each and every property. This keeps you from buying a property that eventually becomes more hassle than it is worth. As a matter of fact, successful investors use a system whether they are buying their first or their hundredth property.

Let's look at how easy this can be. Say you want to buy a piece of property. You know, through media stories, that a particular city is economically strong and marked for steady improvement. Still, you're bothered by the naysayers. They exist in all market conditions and your job is to learn how to get to the truth instead of reacting to opinion. Instead of allowing someone else's negative or positive comments to dictate your actions, you decide to investigate the situation yourself. You apply the ACRE program and start investigating. You then talk to others who are already investing in the region (a good place to find them is at the community forums at www.myREINspace.com), and they tell you they use 10 economic fundamentals to analyze the direction real estate values are poised to take in a target area.

Those 10 fundamentals are the foundation of Chapter One. To recap, they cover passive economic fundamentals (mortgage interest rates; changes in average incomes; increased in-migration/demand; the ripple effect; local, regional and provincial economic climate; transportation corridor expansion; and gentrification) and the active economic fundamentals (creating highest and best use; buy wholesale, sell retail; quality marketing). When you make these economic fundamentals part of your system, you confirm their role in the decisions you make. You do not need to have every fundamental work in your favour, but if the passive fundamentals are working against your business, expect trouble.

## First Step: Information and Analysis

Sophisticated investors would consider analysis of these fundamentals as the foundation of their due diligence program and, in fact, their real estate investment business. They know that even when a majority of the 10 fundamentals overwhelmingly favours real estate investment in a particular area, this data only skims the surface of the buy and sell decisions they need to make. Once they identify a community or city where real estate investment appears to make sense, they drill deeper.

Knowing that a successful investor makes money when they buy the right investment property (and loses money when they buy the wrong one), they focus their due diligence on figuring out if a property works for their portfolio. Using REIN's All Properties Due Diligence Checklist, they then apply their investor mentality to find out the facts specific to the property.

You can quickly see that a review of the specific property comes second in line for strategic investors. Armed with solid data about the local economy and real estate market, the system helps them make sure they do not sugarcoat the property analysis. They are honest with themselves about deferred maintenance repairs, appliance purchases, renovation costs, taxes and what they can do to increase rent. They fill out a REIN Property Analyzer to ascertain whether monthly rent surpasses monthly expenses. If it does not create positive income (no matter how great the property looks), they go elsewhere. The investor mentality remains focused on annual cash flow and yield as opposed to acquiring a property that takes money out of their pockets every month with only the promise of a potential property value increase. In terms of portfolio growth, quality beats quantity—every time.

## Second Step: More Due Diligence

As part of that focus on annual cash flow and yield, sophisticated investors continue to follow their system. The quality of the acquisition, rather than the speed with which it is acquired, is what matters most.

In addition to learning about when and where to buy, the savvy investors cultivate relationships as part of their due diligence. They get to know realtors who are knowledgeable about specific geographic regions and property styles, and are interested in working with investors. Many realtors prefer not to work with investors, but a select group understand that it is more profitable to work with people who buy properties more often than homeowners who buy and sell a property once every five years, on average.

Strategic investors also line up their proposed lenders in advance of finding the property and they analyze their sources of down payment (whether it's their own capital, joint-venture money or from a line of credit) and closing costs. This preliminary work takes the pressure off the transaction and allows them to act quickly when the proper deal is uncovered. The opposite is often true for the non-strategic investor. These individuals focus on the property first. When they find a property they want, they find themselves under substantial and unnecessary stress as they try to line up all of the pieces to make the deal come together. Too many wild cards exist in the purchase process to nail down after the property is found. No wonder non-strategic investors are often identified as *struggling* investors!

It must be said that roadblocks exist at nearly every turn in the real estate investment process. But few are real surprises. Sophisticated investors get used to encountering roadblocks and manage the obvious ones in advance. When confronted with the unexpected, they look behind the curtain to solve the problem so they can get on with their business. They find out how to fix partner credit or financing issues (and in the future, they check them out first!). They take the data generated by the property appraiser and complete their own cash flow analysis. They credit their system for helping them make sure a deal doesn't close until after they have all of the information they need to make an informed decision.

───────────────────── ∿ ─────────────────────

**You would never want your pilot to skip steps on his checklist, because that would represent too much of a risk, even if the pilot was highly experienced. Strategic investors take investing just as seriously and never skip a step on their checklist—even when their instincts tell them to do so.**

─────────────────────────────────────────────

A sophisticated investor mentality demands that one take responsibility for one's own due diligence at every stage of the investment process. Landlord–tenant relationships are complicated. Lease-to-own and joint-venture deals require legally binding agreements the investor can turn to if lessees or money partners decide they want out of a property early. Again, a quality investment system compels the investor to take these steps. No flying by the seat of their pants. It also acknowledges that skipping steps is the same as willfully adding risk. I always have checklists and stick closely to proven systems for all aspects of the business. Follow my example and your brain is free to be ultra-creative in structuring deals that build your portfolio. Checklists don't box you in. They are catalysts for creativity.

## A View from the Trenches

Problems with the landlord–tenant relationship tend to generate a lot of angst for new and experienced investors. In the spring of 2012, CBC Radio carried several news stories about rogue relationships that cost landlords big bucks. These stories frustrate me. Believe it or not, a lot of my frustration is directed less at bad tenants than at landlords who find themselves ill-prepared to deal with them.

In dealing with rental properties, defense is the best offense. I advocate a somewhat radical approach, one that acknowledges that tenants are *essential* to my business plan because they pay my mortgages and they take care of my investments. In return for holding up their end of that equation, I provide them with a quality place to live. I am committed to my role in that partnership. But if they renege on their role, we're done, and I will work quickly to end the relationship.

My central point is that tenant selection requires a good deal of attention. Sadly, when some investors have a suite that stays vacant for more than a month, they start to panic. They think they have to put anyone in the suite, just to get the next month's rent, and lower their tenant standards to achieve that result. That's not strategic. The decision often leads to later heartache and the loss of a much larger sum of money thanks to the hassles involved in the tenant eviction process.

---  ∼  ---

**Decisions made in desperation often
lead to desperate situations.**

---

Short-term concern over a vacant rental suite does not lead a sophisticated investor to deviate from a diligent selection process. Tenants can be thoroughly vetted. Leases can spell out exactly when and how rent is to be delivered and what happens if it is late. The specific terms of move-in and move-out inspections can be laid out in advance. The eviction process, which protects your investment, should be planned in advance. If the details of how to put any of these points into action elude you, make it your business to replace your ignorance with information. (The Authentic Canadian Real Estate System, as detailed in my book *Real Estate Investing in Canada 2.0: Creating Wealth with the ACRE System* is a good place to start. REIN's home study course, Landlording Secrets: The Definitive Tenant and Property Management System, is another. The latter spells out your due diligence with templates like the Renovation "Rent Ready" Checklist, Instant Rental Approval Form, Landlord's Hospitality Checklist for New Tenants, Basic Residential Lease Agreement and much more!)

Remember: the investor mentality views tenants as our customers. This changes the dynamic between you and the tenant and you find ways to make the relationship work over the long term.

## Beware the Powerful, Unfounded Motivators

New investors sometimes confuse my enthusiasm for their early successes with my position that investors must take emotion out of their decision-making process. So let me be clear: real estate investors should celebrate their acquisitions and their sales. This is a long-term journey to success, so don't wait until the end to celebrate your achievements. Give yourself and your team that proverbial pat on the back for accomplishments along the way. Following a system isn't designed to take the glory out of life. It is meant to add freedom, so the journey is more enjoyable and ultimately more successful financially.

Fear and greed are the emotions the system is designed to mitigate. Fear stems from ignorance and it can lead investors to buy the wrong property *(What if one gets away?)*, accept the wrong tenants *(What if that property sits vacant?)* or change an exit strategy because they fear losing a co-venturer or because they can't sleep at night because they're haunted by naysayers who are convinced the real estate sky is about to fall on their heads.

Sophisticated real estate investors understand that fear is a powerful motivator. It is also easy to recognize, because the action it dictates cannot be traced back to one's investment system.

Greed is more complicated—and just as dangerous. Fear encourages us to doubt our investment system and take risky actions, even though all of the checklists and analyses say we should not do what fear encourages. Instead of analyzing the facts dispassionately, we act as if the facts don't matter.

---

**Greed encourages us to think we know more than our investment system.**

---

Here, the facts don't matter because there is no way to measure what the investor *knows* to be true. At the height of the real estate boom in 2006 and 2007, I heard Canadian investors make statements such as the following:

- "Sure it has negative cash flow, but I'll make money when I sell."
- "Buy high, sell higher. This market can't go down."
- "Cheap is good. I don't need classy tenants."
- "I can always find a buyer for my properties."

These are not the statements of sophisticated investors with a healthy and wise investor mentality. They are the statements of speculators. Speculators make money, but at what cost of added risk? They also lose money when they hit an economic bump on the road (and there will always be bumps!).

## The Importance of Following Through

The investor mentality helps investors understand that problems need solutions. Real estate investors take responsibility for finding the solutions that work for their portfolio, rather than complaining about their situation. Guided by the data gleaned from the due diligence outlined in their investment system, they effectively train themselves to make success a habit—and that's what following through is all about. Will you make mistakes? For sure (and I certainly did). But if you understand why you're investing in real estate you will also stay the course, learn from your mistakes and profit over the long run.

In sum real estate investment is a *thinking* person's business and it demands action. But this is not rocket science and you do not need to qualify for Mensa or have a university degree to do incredibly well. As investors acquire experience and expertise, they will:

1. know what to do when confronted by different market conditions;
2. learn how to recognize when market conditions are changing or poised for change; and
3. make success a habit, regardless of whether they're consolidating or expanding a portfolio or putting exit strategies into play.

## Pocket Gold

The Sophisticated Investor Binder is another valuable take-home tool ACRE puts directly into the hands of real estate investors. The binder outlines who you are as investor and tells lenders how you intend to pay back a mortgage loan. It includes a cover letter, proof of income, a completed and signed application, a personal cash flow summary, credit bureau report, net worth statement and a revenue real estate asset statement.

Assemble this information as part of your early due diligence, long before you even find a property, then optimize its value by putting it in a binder you can share with lenders and prospective money partners.

# Chapter Six

# Riding the Cycle to Long-Term Sustainable Wealth

~

I LOVE LISTENING TO PEOPLE talk about what they would buy—if only they could. That's probably why I smile every time I hear that BNL classic, *If I Had a Million Dollars*. People who are serious about creating wealth take note: real estate is a viable route to long-term sustainable wealth.

Riding a bicycle is one way to increase your physical fitness and improve your chances of living a long and healthy life. Of course, jumping on a bike for the first time in years and sprinting at an Olympic pace can have exactly the opposite effect, making you unwell to the point at which you require resuscitation. That is why slow and steady progress over a few years—giving you time to build up to Olympic sprint levels—is so critical.

The same rule can be applied to riding the real estate cycle. Building your portfolio slowly and steadily, rather than pushing for explosive growth all at once, can lead to your achieving the equivalent of an Olympic level financial goal. Building it fast and furiously, however, can lead to catastrophic financial and emotional issues.

Finding the right portfolio growth speed is one of the foundational pieces to long-term sustainable wealth creation. For some who have a strong financial background, that pace may be quite quick. For others, just getting started on the journey of taking control of their financial future demands a pace that is a little slower and more methodical. The chosen pace is only right or wrong to the extent that it meets the individual investor's goals, strategies and abilities. Indeed, portfolio growth happens quite organically once an investor allows his system to guide his decisions. I am not suggesting that portfolios can (or should!) expand quickly. I am saying that strategic investors who allow themselves to be guided by a proven system that tells them what to do—and when to do it—will find it relatively easy to turn their attention to the specifics of what must be done.

## Beware of the Black Swans

Before I explore the specifics of portfolio growth, let's revisit an important point about the reality of the real estate cycle. As stated earlier in this book, systems and up-to-date market data are essential components of the risk-mitigation tools that strategic investors use when building a portfolio. But even with the best systems, one cannot ignore the Black Swans that show up announced. Made popular by Nassim Nicholas Taleb in his book, *The Black Swan: The Impact of the Highly Improbable*, this rare bird is a metaphor for unforeseen events that affect a plan. He describes these events as:

> an event with the following three attributes.
>
> First, it is an outlier, as it lies outside the realm of regular expectations, because nothing in the past can convincingly point to its possibility.
>
> Second, it carries an extreme impact.
>
> Third, in spite of its outlier status, after the fact it is often inappropriately rationalized with the benefit of hindsight.

Examples of recent Black Swans include civil unrest in the Middle East, the spread of bird flu, major droughts, the

World Trade Center attack of September 11, 2001 and banking fraud driven by the recession. Knowing they exist and can show up at any time is a strong argument in favour of a strategic investor's goal of mitigating risk by building a portfolio slowly and methodically for greater stability.

Strategic investors also remember that Black Swans do not affect every region the same way. When SARS hit Ontario, it stopped much of that province's economy in its tracks, but

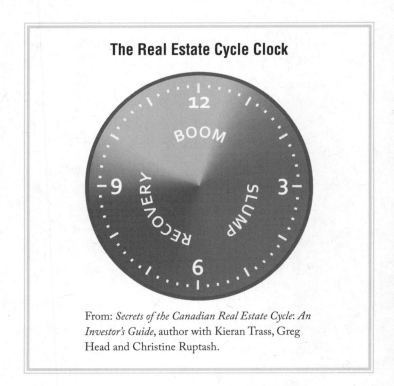

**The Real Estate Cycle Clock**

From: *Secrets of the Canadian Real Estate Cycle: An Investor's Guide*, author with Kieran Trass, Greg Head and Christine Ruptash.

other regions of North America were largely unaffected. The same thing occurred in 2008. While the global recession hit Europe and the United States extremely hard, its impact was fairly short-lived and not as deep in Canada.

When the 2008 crisis hit, many strategic Canadian real estate investors could see the impending market shift from boom to slump and responded by modifying their tactics. They became more proactive in portfolio management, which is one of the key tactics sophisticated investors employ during an economic downturn.

Less-strategic investors reacted emotionally. Because they were ill-prepared, either emotionally or mentally, for an economic slowdown, some divested their portfolios at great speed and at exactly the wrong moment in the cycle. They improperly extrapolated problems occurring in other regions of the world all the way down to the property they held in locations such as Thunder Bay. They made decisions based on fear, not fact. Strategic investors acted differently. Understanding that regional real estate markets move in cycles that are largely independent of global swings, they shifted their tactics to match market conditions. The other group misinterpreted signals about the shifting market, effectively losing their investor mentality when they panicked. Many members of this non-strategic cohort experienced great financial loss and emotional distress because they made their moves at exactly the wrong time in the cycle. Instead of acting strategically, they followed the crowd.

---

**Acting in step with the market cycle,
strategic investors reviewed their
portfolios and took proactive steps
to further mitigate their risk.**

---

Some savvy investors downsized by getting rid of speculative or underperforming properties. Others looked for ways to strengthen their marketing to attract and keep quality tenants, at the same time reviewing their operations, looking for possible savings.

---

**During a slump the strategic investor
gets proactive while an emotional
investor hides his head in the sand.**

---

Contrary to what the less-strategic masses were doing, some sophisticated investors analyzed market fundamentals that favoured rental markets and expanded their holdings by buying the investment properties others were selling at a deep discount. (Market prices rise as a recovery takes root, but decline in a slump.)

Those who opted to vacate the market as soon as possible were obviously guided (or misguided) by an emotional (fearful) response. But what about sophisticated investors who chose to take remarkably *different* actions? Some consolidated their portfolios or changed their management practices. Others took advantage of falling market values and expanded their portfolios by buying more revenue properties in regions where the economic fundamentals had barely shifted in response to global concerns. Still others did a bit of both. Were any of these strategic investors shrewder than others?

As an industry insider, I can tell you there is no one right answer when it comes to dealing with market shifts and Black Swans. Indeed, I was intrigued to see how individual investors took the same information and employed different tactics to help them survive the economic turbulence that started in 2008. As a group, strategic investors understand that there is no benefit to jumping in and out of this business (or any business, for that matter). Since their goals are long-term and their profits are created over long-term cycles, they analyze market shifts without sacrificing their goals—or the systems they have put in place to achieve those goals. Talk about being *intentional* and *strategic*! These investors allowed their systems to level out some of the potentially negative implications that could otherwise result from the inevitable ups and downs of the market. More than anything, their tactics epitomize a commitment to long-term sustainable wealth.

## Keeping in Step

To learn more about portfolio management that keeps in step with changes in the real estate cycle, read my book (with Kieran Trass, Greg Head and Christine Ruptash), *Secrets of the Canadian Real Estate Cycle: An Investor's Guide*. It helps readers understand and analyze market cycles so they can better use market data to invest for portfolio growth.

## The Beauty of Leverage

Financial leverage, a.k.a. borrowed money, makes the real estate wheel go around. But it's terribly shortsighted to think that leverage is all about money. Sophisticated investors know that money is only one element you can leverage. Yes, you need money to close deals. And money—regardless of whether it's from cash flow, partners or mortgages—definitely attracts more money.

But leverage, in its purest sense, is really about knowledge. It's about who you have surrounded yourself with, their knowledge base and what you bring to the relationship that they can leverage. Knowledge, information and contacts are the other three elements a strategic investor leverages, and none of these can be used effectively unless you surround yourself with other legitimate investors.

---

### Strategic Leveraging

A sophisticated investor leverages knowledge, information and contacts.

- **Knowledge:** A working knowledge of the strategies and tactics used to create wealth in real estate can be shared and leveraged by working with other legitimate investors, including money partners. This mitigates risk by helping investors avoid financial pitfalls.
- **Information:** Strategic investors leverage the information of others to gather unbiased and unemotional information on economics, regions, neighbourhoods and properties. Working with trusted sources is the quickest and most effective way to access quality information. Tim Hortons and Walmart don't open stores without doing extensive market research and neither should you. The good news is you don't have to do it all yourself.
- **Contacts:** Building a trusted team (see Chapter 4) lessens your portfolio risk while saving you time and energy. Strategic investors leverage other investors' contacts while sharing their own, thus strengthening their team and building future contacts.

## Financial Leverage

Whether they're buying property for business or personal use, most investors will find themselves talking to a lender about a mortgage. In the simplest terms, the borrower leverages a certain amount of his own capital in return for a loan (private or institutional) on a real property purchase. That is why building solid relationships within the financing community is an important step for investors.

------------------------------ ∼ ------------------------------

**Real estate investors benefit from their relationship
with the financial partners because it gives them
an opportunity to profit from the full value of
the property even though they put only a small
portion of their own money into the deal.**

------------------------------------------------------------

The power of financial leverage is best explained by example. To keep it simple, let's say an investor puts up $200,000 of her own money to buy an investment property. If that property increases in value by 5 per cent ($210,000), the return on investment (ROI) would be 5 per cent. If that same investor leverages the purchase price by using just $40,000 of her own money and borrows $160,000 from the bank, that 5 per cent ROI now escalates to 25 per cent, because the tenant pays the cost of interest. This is in stark contrast to stock market returns. There, a 5 per cent increase in most cases tallies 5 per cent, period.

This example does not dismiss the reality that borrowed money must be paid back. On the contrary, a sound investment system ensures that the rent collected from the property will pay for itself, including the mortgage payment.

Given the potential to leverage borrowed money, the sophisticated real estate investor quickly learns to view his lender as his best partner. He also understand that not all lenders are institutions, and not all institutions are the same or have the same policies. Each bank has its own set of rules and each of these rules can change at a moment's notice. Non-bank institutional lenders such as MCAP are mostly governed by whatever rules the Canada Mortgage and Housing Corporation (CMHC) is operating under, even if the loan does not meet the threshold for insurance.

Credit unions, on the other hand, are not covered under the Bank Act and therefore are able to be more flexible. Good credit unions are becoming more important players in the strategic investors' world. Although most conventional real estate purchases involve institutional lenders, there is a variety of circumstances where private loans make sense. Indeed, while successful investors build their portfolios by sharing risk and ownership with joint venture equity partners, others use private lenders to kick-start a purchase or to bridge a short-term financing gap while still keeping full ownership of the property. Although the interest rate may seem high, it is often still less expensive than giving up 50 per cent of the property's equity appreciation and cash flow to a joint-venture partner.

For example, those who buy a discounted property with a plan to renovate the property and either quickly resell it or refinance it often find the use of private lenders works well. Here, a short-term loan at 12 per cent interest may work better than a less-flexible bank's 4 per cent deal. In fact, many regular institutions do not like making these short-term mortgages and make it difficult to get approval. In cases like that, strategic investors leverage their knowledge, information and contacts to access the funds that fit the specific tactic.

This kind of arrangement at the front-end of a property investment gives the real estate expert several options in terms of a longer-term strategy. For example, a strategic investor may borrow from a private source to give himself time to turn a poorly-managed revenue property into a well-managed site with full suites and quality tenants. An investor could use private capital to launch this investment and then pay back the higher-cost capital (with interest) when the property is performing at its best. Once that occurs, the investment will be attractive to a regular institution that offers much lower interest rates. A real estate investor may also use private cash to turn the property around and then use another partner's cash to buy out the loan, with the second co-venturer entering the deal as part of a longer-term buy-and-hold strategy with the real estate expert. The real estate investor could also buy out the private loan and maintain 100 per cent ownership once the property was operational.

———————————— ∾ ————————————

**The raw beauty of the private loan is that the investor maintains ownership of 100 per cent of the property.**

This has some obvious profit advantages upon property disposition. That said, investors who think that leverage is all about your own or private money will miss key opportunities to expand their portfolios.

## Financial Partner's Money

While some real estate investors focus on private loans or their own capital to build their portfolios, most do not. Instead, they leverage a co-venturer's ability to borrow capital from traditional financial institutions. The most common of these deals involve a 50:50 partnership in which a joint-venture partner puts up the capital for the down payment. The partners share ownership, with the real estate expert (there's that word again!) doing all of the work associated with finding, managing and eventually selling the property.

Profits are shared 50:50 after the initial down payment is returned to the co-venturer.

Again, this strategy says as much about relationships as it does about money. This is why successful real estate investors who build their portfolios using what they call "other people's money" insist that finding joint-venture (JV) capital is easy. By focusing on strong relationships with members of their investment teams, these individuals build their portfolios using the JV money of people they already know. In many cases, these people come from the investor's inner circle of contacts. They are family members, friends or co-workers, or have a direct relationship with the investor's family, friends or co-workers. Long before the first JV deal closes, these individuals already have some kind of a track record with the real estate expert.

To learn more about how sophisticated investors translate their personal and business relationships into real estate co-ventures, take REIN's home study course, JV Secrets, or read my bestselling book (with Russell Westcott), *Real Estate Joint Ventures: The Canadian Investor's Guide to Raising Money and Getting Deals Done*. Both provide a step-by-step system for finding, utilizing and maximizing joint-venture money. This strategy works by creating strong relationships in which each party (the investor and the partner) profit by leveraging their assets. The investor leverages his knowledge, information and contacts and the financial partner his access to capital.

———————— ∽ ————————

**This focus on the win-win nature of co-ventured real estate investments is what separates the sophisticated strategist from the more primitive imposter.**

The joint venture is a powerful investment tool, since satisfied money partners tend to come back for more!

## From the Trenches

The Authentic Canadian Real Estate system maintains a sharp focus on using JV money to grow real estate portfolios and many of the best deals fall into the traditional 50:50 model of a JV partnership. Even so, sophisticated investors must keep an open mind about the many ways a JV deal can be put together, especially during uncertain economic times, when money partners may be looking for creative ways to earn investment cash.

Let's say that an investor who's mastered the 50:50 model finds she can't put those deals together as easily as she did before the economic turmoil of 2008. She could let fear of a changed economic landscape distract her from building her portfolio, incorrectly thinking that 50:50 deals are the only ones worth pursuing.

(*continued*)

This approach sells her expansion plans short by keeping her from developing more innovative approaches to her quest for leveraged money. Investors who find themselves in this predicament should review what they know.

If the economic fundamentals are strong and their portfolio is poised to grow, they should continue to look for JV money from people they know, but change the way they use that money. It is possible, for example, to build a portfolio using short-term private loans. Conventional money deals mitigate risk. But private loans can keep you in the driver's seat—and you don't even have to share ownership.

## Leveraging Real Estate Expertise

A lot of investors struggle with the notion of what it means to leverage their real estate expertise. Novice investors worry they don't know enough and veterans forget their advanced knowledge of real estate is what separates them from the pack. So what sets real estate experts apart from others? In addition to having real life investment experience, strategic real estate experts define themselves in three key ways:

1. They are willing to talk about real estate, what they do and how they do it. They don't hold back their supposed "secrets."

2. They act with confidence, credibility and integrity.
3. They under-promise and over-deliver.

## Turn All Conversations to Real Estate

The real estate expert doesn't want to bore people with the details of what he does. But whether he's investing part-time or full-time, the strategic investor understands the intrinsic value of being able to *turn all conversations to real estate*—without selling.

Remember what I said above about the value of the investor's relationships and inner circle? Sophisticated real estate investors who are serious about growing their portfolios with the outcome of long-term sustainable wealth are like any other proud business owner: they talk to people about what they do and how they do it. By willingly sharing stories about their experiences, they *tell* rather than *sell* the deal. This helps build that inner circle of potential partners and contacts.

The less-strategic investors are often of two camps. Members of one group are too reticent and perhaps even embarrassed that they are real estate investors. Consequently, they choose not to talk to anyone about what they do. Members of the second group are so aggressive that when-ever they talk about their investments they become like pushy salesmen and make everyone around them uncom-fortable. Neither of these approaches would be successful in any business or profession (unless, of course, they are selling food slicers at the local fair) so it's not surprising they don't work in the investment real estate realm either.

Strategic investors know the calm and sophisticated approach is best because their inner circles, when combined with the inner circles of their family, friends and co-workers, give them incredible access to potential partners, some interested only in private loans, others in co-venturing on revenue properties.

To find co-venturers within those circles, investors practise doing what it takes to *turn all conversations to real estate*. They do not shy away from questions about what they do, how they do it and how it benefits their money partners. When conversations take a more businesslike edge, these investors set up meetings to go over the details in a more formal—and professional—environment. As real estate *experts* they will do what it takes to show others that they know what they're talking about. Again, it's all about telling, not selling.

The bottom line is that strategic investors know they must become the person who attracts working capital. They constantly ask, "If I was approached with this deal in the manner I just approached this prospect, would I lend this individual money to buy revenue property?" The real answer to the question lies in the result: if no cheques come in, then the answer is obvious and changes must be made.

The investor who is serious about building long-term sustainable wealth appreciates that question because she knows it can lead to more fruitful discussions of specific real estate investments. She is okay with the question because she knows she can answer it: her response always comes from her proven system and her commitment to mutually beneficial investments.

---

### Just the Facts

Always put yourself in your prospects' shoes and look at the deal, the approach, the finances and the presentation from their point of view. If you are honest in your assessment of what it looks like to *them*, you will be pleasantly surprised at how easy it is to spot the positive changes that you need to make.

Become the person you would gladly invest $100,000 with if you were approached by that individual.

---

## The CCI Index

This willingness to *turn all conversations to real estate* is an extension of the CCI Index discussed in Chapter Five. In sum, an investor with a high CCI IQ knows what he's talking about and is committed to acting ethically and legally.

He *turns all conversation to real estate* because he recognizes that his investments offer mutually-beneficial financial opportunities. The fact that the vast majority of his money partners will always be individuals with whom he already has a relationship is a definite bonus. Who doesn't want to work with people you already know and like?

## Portfolio Strength: Marketing and Management

Investors who are serious about growing their portfolios soon recognize that their most important marketing tools all come back to evidence of their investment success. Buying the right properties is critical—but it's closely followed by the need to manage those properties for investment success. This is the meat and potatoes of why JV partners will be attracted to your investments.

Strategic investors recognize that quality investments only perform if they have high-quality marketing and property management. The first focuses on keeping suites full or finding the right buyers for properties that are for sale. Marketing is definitely part of property management. I've noted it separately because non-strategic investors often fail to give marketing its due. They think they're struggling with cash flow and the need to master budget contingencies when their real problem is rooted in the fact that their suites are not rented. That sounds trite, but it's true. It's comparable to not being able to see the forest for the trees!

Quality property management should always include a marketing component. But marketing is never an end in itself. For most investors, marketing is all about getting quality tenants into quality suites—and that emphasis on *quality* is key. The raw beauty of real estate investing is that properties that produce cash flow enable your clients (tenants) to pay your debt and enhance your long-term financial security. Strategic investors take that very seriously.

Again, a healthy property contributes to a healthy portfolio, which improves your ability to capitalize on future wealth. Ignore property management, or undervalue its contribution to your portfolio's strength, and you play Russian roulette with your future.

## Don't let Unqualified Media Noise Influence Your Investment Decisions

Portfolio strength is one of the best ways to bring JV partners into your investment business. Money partners are attracted by proven success. That proven track record can be compromised by misinformation.

The introduction to this chapter alluded to one of the biggest problems new and experienced investors encounter: confusion about what the real estate market cycle is and how it impacts investment portfolios. This confusion is compounded by what I call "unqualified media noise," which can greatly complicate an investor's ability to establish himself as an expert.

To be clear, professional media can be an excellent source of information about what's happening in local, national and global economies. But with the advent of the internet, many unqualified voices also make themselves heard and bombard investors with a lot of erroneous noise. The end result is that all the sometimes contradictory and misguided information leaves non-investors confused. To avoid a similar fate, strategic investors must develop a filter that focuses on trusted and unbiased sources with strong real estate investment fundamentals and experience. There is no time to listen to theorists who just restate scraps and tidbits they've heard. A good example of how erroneous information can cloud decisions is embodied by a common assessment of the 2008 recession. Those who say it was the worst since the Great Depression add negative fuel to the information fire. In reality, that recession isn't even the second-worst in Canada; it's the third-worst. When the constant repetition of that mistruth entered the common psyche, it left a majority of Canadian convinced this was the worst recession in Canadian history. Known as an "availability heuristic," myths such as this feed a very powerful thought process that becomes dangerous in its ability simultaneously to be easy to remember—and wrong! Strategic investors must continually fight to avoid getting caught in similar traps. Those who manage to do that are able to see the market with a clarity that few others share!

Potential money partners without that expertise in real estate may be so confused and caught up in an availability heuristic that they cannot get past it, even when strategic investors try to share real truth.

———————————— ∼ ————————————

**The confusion caused by unqualified media noise is calmed by strategic real estate experts who can help their partners negotiate the difference between the distracting babble and market fundamentals. These investors understand that making money in real estate comes down to the difference between knowing what you're talking about—and guessing.**

A strategic investor will also explain to his money partners and potential money partners that the vast majority of headlines are designed to sell media, not to provide unbiased facts and figures. A renter who is thinking about buying a home may listen to news of interest rate increases and decide to keep renting, a fact that might impact the local housing market. An investor may hear the same news and be excited about the fact that higher rates stabilize his target area's rental pool. Similarly, home buyers can fall in love with a property. Conversely, the investor falls in love with numbers—not a great kitchen or bathroom!

## Separating E-Facts and E-Fiction

Confusion about what the media noise means is amplified by the current proliferation of misinformation in what some call the "Age of Protest." Fuelled by access to the internet, which provides a cheap but massive platform to even the most ignorant or biased among us, discussions abound of real estate markets, booms, busts and bubbles.

Fortunately for the real estate investment business, that debate often happens well outside the circles frequented by strategic investors. The strategic investor should stay out of the fray. He knows that his portfolio performance is dependent on the relationships he builds with people who are in his inner circle, where his non-real estate related relationships have already engendered relationships based on mutual respect and trust. The strategic investor becomes the go-to person for people with questions about real estate and when these individuals see how the expert uses facts and fundamentals to address their concerns or queries, they listen more closely to his ideas.

Again, success in real estate is about building portfolio strength based on market fundamentals. It is about the facts, not guesswork.

---

## Just the Facts

With so many Canadians disappointed by the meagre returns offered by many investments, questions about real estate investment are an excellent opportunity to show others that you know what you're talking about. No matter what the question, I encourage strategic investors to use it as a way to establish their real estate expertise. Remember: you never know who's listening!

Here are some of the key points your answers should cover:

- I invest based on my own analysis of proven real estate fundamentals.
- This is why I focus on a particular geographic area.
- I follow a system that values the importance of cash flow.
- I know how to put different kinds of investments to work (private loan or co-ownership).
- I focus on certain tactics (rent-to-own, buy-and-hold, fix-and-flip).
- I am committed to win-win property investments.

## How to Work with Partners

Finding money partners can be easier than working with them, but the strategic investor uses knowledge to navigate his way around potential landmines. By applying the same level of due diligence to partner evaluations that they'd apply to property searches, sophisticated investors bring new partners into their property investments without compromising long-term financial goals.

For a primer on working with JV partners, check out my book, *Real Estate Investing in Canada 2.0*. A more advanced discussion of how to put together solid JV deals is detailed in my book (with Russell Westcott), *Real Estate Joint Ventures: The Canadian Investor's Guide to Raising Money and Getting Deals Done*. The most important point to remember is that you do not need to work with everyone who wants a piece of your investment pie. The people you choose to work with must be qualified to be there—and your system can help you identify them because it troubleshoots potential problems, including many that new investors may not immediately recognize.

The joint ventures secrets book, for example, walks investors through everything, from how to generate JV leads, to the application of the principles of wealth-attraction and how to filter potential money partners to make sure you can work together. The system also covers how to structure JV deals and the essentials of what must be included in a legally binding JV agreement.

The strict application of so much upfront due diligence explains why few strategic investors ever revisit formal JV agreements. When so much attention is paid to how these deals are structured, they rarely unravel.

## Pocket Gold

Sophisticated real estate investors aim to be strategic and intentional—and they let that approach guide their decisions. Below is a list of some of the strategies smart investors use to deal with market uncertainties. As you read through them, think about how you could communicate this information to prospective money partners. These are solid examples of your real estate expertise.

- **Interest rates.** Analyze your properties with an interest rate that's 1 per cent higher than today's rate.
- **Job growth.** Ignore national figures, focus on your target region and how it is being affected. Sustained unemployment is high in some parts of the country. Focus on regions with persistent job growth and jobs created by projects with multi-year timelines. These jobs will stay in place even with shifts in

*(continued)*

commodity prices and demand. They also attract a majority of workers from outside the region. Investors call these workers "renters."

- **The European factor.** Global investors (including Canadians) see the upside of a stable economy but the money they're putting into Canadian real estate, especially in major centres like Toronto and Vancouver, can definitely skew the market. The sophisticated investor avoids overheated markets—and follows job and population growth instead.

- **Markets heat. Markets cool.** Overheated markets eventually cool down. Seasoned investors watch for the strategic advantages offered by cooling markets (think: motivated vendors and dropping prices). They also watch for the economic fundamentals that will sustain long-term growth. What happens when people lose confidence in the real estate market? They become renters.

- **Strategy wins.** Knowledge and strategy always trump emotions and guesswork.

# Chapter Seven

# Why Do You Really and Truly Want to Invest in Real Estate?

WHENEVER I HEAR BON JOVI SING, *Welcome to Wherever You Are*, it makes me think about how real estate investment means different things to different people. I've met a lot of Canadians who have been very successful in real estate investment. Some of them are full-time investors who own hundreds of units in large multi-family complexes. Others keep working at their job while owning a couple (or a couple of dozen) revenue properties that provide them that extra monthly income they need to have a better life. Many others are now living their dream. Having achieved what they wanted with their strategic real estate investing, they are living off their cash flow, sailing for months at a time, travelling to help charities, driving the hottest car in town—whatever they want to do with their money.

I have also met many who have not made it through a typical real estate cycle. They got into the business without a realistic plan, and they didn't understand that real estate investing requires attention to detail and awareness of its inevitable ups and down. Members of this cohort got caught up in the get-rich myth that surrounds real estate investing and forgot all about it being a business that takes proactive management and analysis. This type of people can be found in any and all industries, investments and walks of life—so it's no surprise real estate investing attracts them, too.

In this book, you have discovered that true long-term success in real estate is created by having a proven system to follow. Of course, success varies from one individual to another.

---

**Success in real estate can only be measured by what it is that each individual investor sets out to achieve.**

---

Success really is different for all people at all times. Some investors just want to make enough extra cash to build a nest egg that will be a small or modest part of their long-term financial strategy. Others want to build a giant legacy that positively affects their lives as well as many others. There is no right or wrong goal, or any single way to measure success.

The one component of real estate success that doesn't waver is quality. The quality of your real estate investments are far more important than the speed at which your portfolio grows. It doesn't matter if you are investing to create a full-time endeavour or if you just want to augment other financial strategies. The quality of the property and the region in which it is located are the most critical pieces of the long-term puzzle.

For example, a lot of middle-aged investors see part-time real estate investment as a way to feather supplement their retirement nests. Regardless of why they get started, all are attracted by the opportunity to earn passive income with a potential for capital appreciation. Their end goals differ because they are working with different visions of what their future will look like. But, whatever their goals, nothing will be achieved if a property is bought on speculation because it is cheap or if it is purchased in a region with a past rather than a future.

Regardless of an investor's specific goal, at REIN, we call this quest for a certain quality of life a Personal Belize, as in:

What's your Personal Belize? I first introduced this concept in my book, *Real Estate Investing in Canada 2.0: Creating Wealth with the ACRE System*. While the term connotes visions of sandy beaches and tropical sunshine, we never expect one Personal Belize to look like another. What we do expect is that every Personal Belize will have its roots in the same quest: future financial security through sophisticated real estate investment. Once you're in a room with a bunch of people for whom that's a shared goal, good things happen!

## A Portfolio with Purpose

I have written extensively in this book about how sophisticated investors build future wealth and mitigate risk by being both *strategic* and *intentional*. To summarize the strategic element, REIN teaches the Authentic Canadian Real Estate (ACRE) investment system. ACRE gives investors the tools they need to let real estate market fundamentals, not guesses or sales pitches, guide their investment decisions. The system provides investors with the exact questions to ask, the answers they should be receiving and the tools to dig deeper than other investors. We do this so that speculation gets thrown out the window and investors truly get their confidence boosted, by looking behind the economic curtain. The system even shows investors how to invite qualified money partners into their investments and then work hard to make sure they are building real estate investment portfolios where they and their joint-venture partners come out on top. These are the major reasons why the REIN system has proven itself in up-and-down markets for over 20 years. It uses successful strategies to generate success.

---

—————————————— ∼ ——————————————

**If the foundation of strategy comes down to knowing what you're talking about and being able to put that knowledge into action, then intentionality is all about doing what you say you'll do.**

---

Sophisticated investors take that notion of intentionality a few steps farther—which is where the Personal Belize really comes into play. These investors don't merely know what they're doing, they know *why* they're doing it. To them, success is much more than a number in a ledger. It is not measured in just dollars earned: it is truly measured by the lifestyle they were shooting for and their ability to obtain it. It is a Personal Belize built on a portfolio with purpose.

## Getting Started

Newcomers to REIN are sometimes surprised to learn that the development of a Personal Belize should be a very early part of their real estate investment journey. Most believe that the best course of action is to jump in, probably because that has been their modus operandi in most aspects of their life: they jump in and fix the problems later. However, when you step back and logically look at all investments, doesn't it make sense to have a real destination in mind rather than a vague idea of "more."

REIN is similar, in a way, to Google Maps. Even if you know where you are starting from, you still need to enter a destination in order for the program to help you get there. For Google it is a geographic destination that needs to be defined. For REIN members and strategic real estate investors, the destination is defined in financial and lifestyle terms. In both cases, the more precision with which you describe your destination, the easier and faster it is to get there. This is why it's so important to understand that a Personal Belize isn't an idealized notion of what future wealth can bring into one's life. It's the detailed description of what you really do plan to do with the wealth you generate.

One of the best ways to start developing your notion of what your Personal Belize will look like is to make a pictorial collage that combines the various components of what financial security will allow you to do. I've seen collages that feature expensive cars, vacation villas and children or grandchildren getting post-secondary education without debt. Other investors paste words such as "mortgage freedom" over photographs of their family homes, or find pictures of exotic locations they plan to visit. I even know a guy whose Personal Belize included a specific cappuccino maker that he wanted installed in the kitchen of his B.C. vacation home. This investor loves spending time with extended family and friends and his definition of a great day begins with a great cup of coffee!

It's very common for investors to develop their Personal Belize around post-retirement plans. Others take a more prosaic approach. Because they may already have suffered the consequences of bad investments, they find comfort in depicting a kind of step-by-step approach to financial freedom. The details of their Personal Belize may change over time, but they will always focus on what they'll be able to do once they meet certain financial goals. For example, they may want to be debt-free in a certain number of years and able to help elderly parents with living expenses, while still putting money aside for their own or their children's future. Or they may want to finance their children's post-secondary education without burdening either their children or themselves with extra debt.

## From the Trenches

I've seen investors run into trouble after pursuing a vision that really belonged to someone else, and that's not a problem I want to promote!

I can tell you that my Personal Belize has strong ties back to the personal vision I wrote when taking

*(continued)*

that business motivational workshop taught by Alan Jacques back in the early 1990s. Imagine what it was like, years later, to realize the ideas expressed in that life-purpose statement also form the crux of my Personal Belize! In short, real estate investment and REIN has enabled me to:

- pursue a future where I can be financially successful while simultaneously helping other people to achieve their own goals;
- help my JV partners generate future wealth;
- mentor thousands of investors—many of whom I only know through the stories other REIN members share with me;
- help my mom and dad when they needed it most;
- travel the country and the world experiencing events my wife Connie and I never thought possible;
- write six bestselling books;
- support a charity we really believe in, Habitat for Humanity. By donating 100 per cent of all my author royalties and combining them with the amazing support of REIN members, we have raised more than $900,000 to build homes for Canadians who need a hand up.

I'm not going to pat myself on the back for this. But I will tell you that a clear understanding of my Personal Belize did a great job of keeping me on track!

## Personal and Professional Goal-Setting

Individual investors must chart their own course. They must also remember that success is in the eye of the beholder. I don't want investors to think they have to want what others have achieved. Indeed, that kind of pursuit says more about emotion than about future wealth—which makes it a very non-sophisticated pursuit. That said, it often makes sense for investors, new and experienced, to ask tough questions about why some of their colleagues are more successful than others. Why are some able to attain their Personal Belize while others struggle? That question is not meant to make investors feel bad. It is meant to reveal where they may need additional assistance to reveal a repetitive flaw in their efforts to pursue long-term wealth. If you are serious about attaining your Personal Belize you must also be serious about how you will go about achieving it.

REIN has plenty of members who use real estate investments to augment their income and net worth. They don't make real estate their life, just as others don't make mutual fund investing their life. That's okay. The primary job of the investment is to make your money work much harder than you so you can achieve what it is you want from life. It is as simple as that. But you must take the time to define what it is you truly want—and guard against letting family, friends or society make you think you must want what they have.

Define what it is you really, truly and honestly want and then make it happen. In other words, take responsibility for what I call personal and professional goal-setting.

——————————— ~ ———————————

**Why take the time to visualize the future that would really make you happy—and then do nothing to achieve it?**

Investors who are serious about their Personal Belize need to ask themselves: how will I measure my own progress as a real estate investor? That's a personal question in that it puts the onus for an answer squarely on your shoulders. Life is a journey, with twists and turns. Your dream or goal may change over time as you and your life situation changes— and that's okay as well. But, as with Google Maps, you must start where you are and at least begin heading in a direction you choose.

I've seen these financial and lifestyle course-changes occur for many different reasons. These shifts can be based on good, bad and even sad news. My life-changing response to my dad's illness is one such example. Because I was able to keep my professional options in step with my personal needs, Connie and I were able to move back to British Columbia and run our portfolio while taking care of my parents. Was that a part of my big life plan at the moment?

Of course not, but because I was already heading in the right financial direction when the detour came, I could make the turn and still have enough gas in the tank to continue on a new route while still heading in the same direction. Thanks to real estate investment, I could pursue meaningful personal goals in a new way!

## Recalibration Is Key to Long-Term Success

The strategic investor also knows he has to recalibrate professional goals with shifts—and impending shifts—in the real estate market, which continually cycles from boom to slump to recovery. The strategic investor who uses market fundamentals to assess the market cycle will find investment opportunities at each phase of that cycle. He will build his portfolio during the recovery phase, capitalize on the boom and adjust in the slump. To do that well, he must be aware of how shifts and impending shifts will impact his ability to achieve his Personal Belize, and adjust his investment tactics accordingly. (The investor who buys during a boom will be over-leveraged for the slump, for example.) The ultimate goals don't change, but the tactics shift to adjust to the new phase of the market cycle.

To stay abreast of market shifts, sophisticated investors continually ask themselves strategic questions about how their portfolios are leveraged. They make it their business to know their loan-to-value ratio and how much credit they could access to buy additional properties or to take a property or properties out of the rental pool for a short period of time so as to improve profitability by marketing a superior product. This is called "stress testing" a portfolio, and it is an integral part of the sophisticated investor's approach to goal-setting. More than anything, it helps investors treat their individual properties like the small businesses they are. Anything less will compromise progress towards the meaningful goals they've identified in their Personal Belize.

## Just the Facts

For a detailed look at how strategic investors stress test their portfolios, I encourage you to read my book (with Kieran Trass, Greg Head and Christine Ruptash), *Secrets of the Canadian Real Estate Cycle: An Investor's Guide*. It provides an in-depth look at why strategic investors ask themselves questions like the following:

- How is my equity goal (read: Personal Belize) impacted by market-value increases or decreases?
- What happens to my cash flow if interest rates rise 0.5 per cent? One per cent?

> • How much additional cash flow can I access if
>   I increase my rents?
> • What happens to my cash flow if vacancies increase?
>
> Armed with answers to questions such as these, inves-
> tors can review their goals and, when needed, switch
> up the tactics they're using to achieve those goals.

This focus on real-world information is a clear extension of
the principles behind the 10 fundamentals outlined by the
REIN investment system. Investors who study the fundamentals use real-world information to make decisions about
the properties they buy. They act with information, not
emotion. The same thing happens when investors stress test
their portfolios to see if they are still on track. Even when
market shifts evoke scary headlines and even scarier on-line
discussions, the strategic investor stays the course. She
understands that market shifts may demand sacrifice—and
it is easier to make sacrifices when you know you are pursuing a meaningful goal!

## Learn to Use Facts to Rule Emotions

Market fundamentals and potential shifts in those fundamentals are essential to understanding the real estate cycle.

This information gives strategic investors a way to deal with a natural fear of failure. It helps investors stay the course even when the waters are rough.

---

**Cash flow + Equity = Future Financial Security**

---

## Giving Back

The best part of my association with REIN is the people I meet. Every REIN event introduces me to new and veteran members of this industry and I am awed when they share news of what real estate investment means for them and their families. Because I remember what it was like to be new to this business, I know that every story of success inspires others to stay the course. Indeed, 51 of those stories are published in detail in my book (with Joy Gregory), *51 Success Stories of Canadian Real Estate Investors*.

The benefit of learning from others who already walk the talk is fundamental to REIN's success. We often tell new members that they are joining an organization that lets them walk in the footsteps of success. They soon discover that they take those steps on the shoulders of giants—a position that really improves an investor's ability to see what's ahead. When you surround yourself with so much first-hand knowledge of how strategic real estate investment works, there is no need to start at step one.

Another factor that makes REIN so spectacular is that it has become a haven for real estate investors whose personal and professional goals include a strong element of giving back. In addition to sharing success stories that routinely bring their fellow REIN members to tears and laughter, these individuals also share the tools they've developed to circumvent common problems. Over the years, that's allowed REIN to build an on-line library of templates for everything from how to qualify a tenant or joint-venture money partner, to JV agreements and landlord–tenant agreements. This willingness to share success saves other members a great deal of money and prevents countless hours of frustration. Why reinvent a wheel when someone else is offering a free ride?

I also appreciate the way so many REIN members, including professional lawyers, accountants, real estate agents and home inspectors, have stepped up to pass on their knowledge to their fellow members. This is why members who can't attend an actual REIN meeting are so keen to receive the audio versions of our events.

After REIN members share this kind of information, either one-on-one or with the larger group, I try to ask them about how it fits with their Personal Belize; I am delighted to say that there is always a connection. Even when a Personal Belize is years away from fruition, strategic investors know that they are laying the foundation of their future life. Because they see personal and professional value in being of service to others, they understand that giving back is about *now* rather than later.

## Pocket Gold

Book some time to begin work on your Personal Belize and then pick some images or items that serve as reminders of where you're headed. Post that item in a visible space (in your office or on your fridge) and use it to remind you of what you're working towards.

Chapter Eight

# Is Real Estate Investing Part of Your Journey?

~

A LOT OF PEOPLE who set out to learn about real estate investing soon reach a point where they find themselves overwhelmed, unable to decide what to do next. They are, as the U2 song goes, *Stuck in a Moment*. That is understandable: embarking on a new direction in life or business always produces some level of anxiety. It's easy to forget that every journey (a new job, friendship, marriage) begins at ground zero, and those first steps are always daunting. However, the result is worth it.

Similarly, casual investors who start on their journey to becoming strategic investors may sometimes hesitate in the early going. They progress from being a little overwhelmed and confused while closing their first few deals and finding the right tenants for their properties to becoming confident and eventually investing with total assurance. An investor never stops learning. Instead, new strategies and tactics are added to her toolkit with every new deal that's done.

Sadly, it is during this journey to becoming a strategic investor that many investors often lose their way. The emotions that cause this are greed and fear. Some will be motivated by greed, and take shortcuts that are costly, and others will be inhibited from acting because of fear. These harmful developments are avoidable, and I want to conclude this book by taking a look at how sophisticated investors steer clear of these minefields.

## Minefield #1: Falling Prey to Greed

Admittedly, there are times when all of us take shortcuts in life—and some of them work out in our favour. But in the world of finance, business and real estate, any potential gains these shortcuts promise must be weighed against a dramatic increase in risk. Often, in fact, the scales that balance risk and reward are tilted in the direction of risk. The short-term wins these shortcuts promise are often at the root of bigger disasters down the road.

Rest assured that I speak from experience. I know it is human nature to be attracted to shortcuts, especially in today's seemingly time-compressed world. But I have seen too many investors compromise their intelligence, education and proven system in an attempt to speed up a process, only to suffer great loss, all in the name of expediency. Most often shortcuts involve cutting corners on due diligence, which then leads to emotion taking control of the decision-making process, which leads to unnecessary risks. Sometimes the shortcut begins with ignoring a legal or bylaw issue. At other times it involves falsifying information on a lending application or simply skipping important analysis. Sometimes the shortcut is all about not taking the time to do background checks on potential joint-venture partners or tenants.

Whatever the shortcut turns out to be, the investor knows better, and yet he willfully ignores the risks. Either laziness or impatience may be to blame. Both are costly. And due to the fact that this let's-speed-up-the-results attitude seems to be hard-wired into many people, industries have sprung up that are devoted to attracting the kind of person who always wants to chase the next big thing. People fall for a sales pitch rather than making a decision based on analysis and hard data.

Strategic investors aren't cynics about new ideas—they're realists. They look for business plans that generate financial success rather than ideas that leave their followers exactly where they started or even farther behind. Real estate investment that creates long-term strategic wealth may lack the emotional excitement of the next big thing, but the results are substantially better.

Indeed, strategic investors understand that the best and most lasting forms of excitement come from results.

---

**When looking to add a little excitement, strategic investors hop on the roller coaster at the local fairground. But when it comes to investing for future financial security, they know that slow and steady are the hallmarks of success.**

---

Sophisticated investors are more than satisfied with following a system that generates long-term wealth. Indeed, it's their end goal!

They also understand that markets are continually shifting and they must adjust their underlying tactics to take advantage of these shifts.

## From the Trenches

Real estate investor Thomas Beyer of Prestigious Properties compares real estate to a satisfying dinner. If this doesn't increase your appetite for real estate investment with a proven system, I don't know what will! According to Thomas:

Real estate is like a three-course meal. The appetiser is the positive cash flow, always appreciated but not required as break-even is okay, too. The main course is the mortgage paydown and it must be there—month after month after month. You will get rich and fat just on the main course. The dessert is the equity appreciation. Like an appetiser, it's always appreciated but not required for a meal or wealth creation.

Unfortunately beginning and inexperienced investors focus *only* on the dessert—and just like in real life, if that is all you eat—you die soon.

To see how this works in real life, do the math. Add a house for $250,000 with $50,000 or 20 per cent down. Assume no cash flow after rent minus all operating expenses and no equity upside. In ten years the mortgage has been paid down (by the tenants) from $200,000 to about 155,000 or by $45,000 (depending on interest

(*continued*)

rates and amortization slightly more or less, of course). By that calculation, you made 90 per cent on the $50,000 invested in ten years, with zero cash flow and zero appreciation. It's better, of course, with dessert and appetizer, but not bad—9 per cent a year on average in a flat market.

Add a modest 2 per cent appreciation per year or only 20 per cent over ten years to this example and you've got another $50,000. That equals another 100 per cent on the cash invested. Some dessert, eh?

## Minefield #2: Falling Prey to Fear

I have also seen investors who look like they're en route to become strategic investors suddenly stop in their tracks. In Minefield #1, the pain comes from going too fast. In Minefield #2 the pain comes from inaction. Investors who succumb to Minefield #2 just do not take the necessary next steps to close on a property. They have all of the same tools at hand that led them to close on properties with solid ROI—so what is happening?

Often it is fear of the unknown or fear of making a mistake. Either way, they're stuck—and many of them aren't able to admit that fear is playing a role in their paralysis; perhaps because they don't recognize what's really happening. More than two decades of experience tells me that even the greenest of newcomers can step into the footsteps of those already investing in the business. What a great feeling to know you can mitigate financial risk by following a proven system. It's like a vicarious hit of confidence.

Fear of failure forces some investors to cling to the safety of the research stage. Some of these would-be investors may never reach the point where they have enough information and get stuck in analysis paralysis for years. Those who can't seem to move forward may give up on their financial dreams, while others will start chasing more get-rich-quick rabbits down the rabbit hole. From fear to greed—yikes!

I sometimes come across people for whom the issue is boredom. Nothing they chase is ever exciting enough. Nothing is worth their time. This is a convenient—and dangerous—point of view, because it completely ignores the fact that fear is what holds them back, not the investment system.

## You Must Cut through the Noise

Never, in the more than 20 years I have studied the Canadian real estate market, has there been so much noise. That's a problem, especially since a little bit of investigation reveals that most of this noise comes from people who have never invested in a single piece of real estate. That's not just sad—it's also dangerous for investors who lack the tools to filter out the information that merits attention from the talking heads who have no business commenting on issues they do not truly understand.

Nassim Nicholas Taleb, in his book, *Antifragile: Things That Gain from Disorder*, points out the importance of differentiating between *signals* and *noise*. His research shows that people make bad decisions when they are overwhelmed by instant information flow (Twitter, Facebook, smartphones, etc.).

---

**The sheer quantity of data confuses the general information flow (noise) with the things that really matter (signals).**

---

Because human beings are hard-wired to protect themselves and the people they care about, those walking through a forest are more likely to believe that a rock in the shadows is a bear (danger) than a bear in the shadows is a rock (and therefore no threat). That same response is why we are drawn to headlines, blog posts and social media that use fear to attract our attention. We are programmed to seek out danger in the information we need to process to get through the day. Those who seek our attention know this and use the knowledge to their advantage, by broadcasting fear, panic and bad news. Your job as a strategic investor is to maintain your perspective and not get manipulated by noisemakers.

The strategic investor has mastered the ability to filter information and distinguish between noise and signals. By focusing on signals, like those that indicate impending shifts in the fundamentals of the market cycle, the sophisticated investor ignores the noise and identifies opportunities. This frees her to recognize real danger signals, like those apparent in economic fundamentals that indicate that a property—or geographic region—is *not* right for her portfolio. In the end, this focus on signals rather than noise keeps us from being caught up in the availability heuristics that the public, or a less-discerning investor, sees as truths. The strategic investor looks behind the curtain.

## Abdication versus Delegation

Once new investors learn how to filter noise from signals and to conquer analysis paralysis, the next danger point they invariably encounter occurs as they make the transition to confident, full-fledged investors. They begin to think that they can be less accountable. There are some investors who begin to skip the critical, and sometimes boring, steps that got them this far in their journey. Once that happens, mistakes begin to creep into their portfolios and they find themselves holding a bad property or working with the wrong team members. This phenomenon occurs often enough that it is important to bring to your attention, whether you are just starting out or have been investing for years.

I personally find it odd that once we start achieving some great results, we are drawn to once again look for shortcuts. If a veteran investor is not careful, he can get drawn back to the same bad habits he had at the beginning of his journey. The problem with rookie mistakes is that they eat into all of the positive results an investor has attained—and the bigger the portfolio the bigger the bite. Why do so many veterans end up on such a dangerous part of the road? The detailed answers can be found in journals and textbooks that look at why people make the same errors over and over again, even when they know better. I think greed is a factor that leads people to take shortcuts. But such actions are also motivated by laziness and ego. Let's be honest. A lot of successful people forget what they did to become successful. They forget how hard they worked. Some even start to think they're too smart to fail. My advice is simple: to avoid this problem in your own real estate investment business, remember what got you to where you are.

—————————————— ∾ ——————————————

**Stick with the strategies that made you successful, even if they begin to feel "beneath" you.**

—————————————————————————————

That's the most productive way to enjoy the journey—and the best way to end up where you want to be.

## Ready, Set, Go!

One of my life missions is to help those who are stuck to get moving again. Investor insiders sometimes call this "getting out of their own way." Once investors learn to get unstuck, I get out of their way because their road—although it will have a few twists and turns—will be a lot smoother. The journey towards their financial goals definitely gets a whole lot easier—and more enjoyable.

## Pocket Gold

### *The Top Reasons to Invest in Real Estate*

Success in real estate comes from doing your homework—
not the type of homework that you were compelled to
do at school, but the type of homework that reduces
your financial risk and sets you up to be financially
secure in a realistic time frame.

It is prudent to talk with current real estate investors
and to ask them why real estate is a large part of their
wealth-creation strategy and life journey. I recently
asked that very question of fellow investors and was
thrilled by their clever—and insightful—responses.
One of the responses came from an investor named
Josie Stern and I like the way it covered so many bases!
Josie wrote:

Real estate is a good investment for the following reasons:

1. It is a more tangible investment, one you can
   actually see, one you can improve to maximize
   return, and overall you are more in control of
   it and the typical investor understands it.
2. Tenants help pay for the mortgage and
   expenses and, after 25 years or so, you will have
   a fully paid-for investment to help with your

retirement. We certainly can't count on the Canada Pension Plan to fund our retirement.

3. If you can't get financing on a single family home, then a multiple family dwelling is a more affordable entry point into the real estate market, which will help you build equity.

4. Historically real estate has delivered strong returns.

If you're looking for more reasons to invest in real estate, ponder the following words of wisdom.

## Opportunity

God's not creating any more Land. Supply and demand say that real estate is a good investment. You can always touch real estate, but can you say the same about your stocks? [It's] much easier to get good information about real estate; companies don't freely share what they are up to.

—Marty Green

Real estate is a "real," tangible, physical asset. A stock simplistically represents a piece of paper that is given its value by someone else's performance, and yet another's analysis and

(*continued*)

accreditation as to what that piece of paper is worth. This phenomenon is way too volatile to be reliable. Real estate has less guesswork and margin for error when you follow a proven system or set of rules for investing. The learning of that system is not beyond the reach of anyone with the desire, gumption and stick-to-it-iveness to learn it. I would rather control my retirement plans than count on a government plan that may or may not be there when I'm ready to retire (or slow down a bit), or take a chance that that stock paper will have enough value at the time I retire.

—Valden Palm

## Investor Control

Because you have control over it.

—Shaun Furman

Freedom. With a strong portfolio I can choose to work, or pack up and move to a new company where I'm happier, or not work at all. Too many people are chained to a job they hate because their families depend on them, but real estate generally gives them more freedom and more control over their lives.

—Steve White

Does not have the anxiety of a day-trade mentality.
—Don R. Campbell

[The] stock investment relies on breaking information and/or what-have-you-done-for-me-lately? scenarios. Real estate, especially as a long-term investment strategy, provides ways that you can succeed regardless of market conditions. If you follow the right formula, and have the right mindset, you can create a cash flow-positive portfolio that brings you financial freedom over time.

In short, if you invest in stocks, you are constantly looking for home runs; if you invest in real estate and follow the correct formula, your portfolio will hit a home run for you.

—Sam Hosseini

You can plan and be sure that it will happen, for the main reason that the control of that plan remains in your hands and not like the stock where the control is out of your hands.

—Ramon Gutierrez

Let's not forget the confidence factor. When you own a piece of real estate, you can see it flourish every year with debt paydown and cash flow (not

(*continued*)

even including appreciation). Then talk to some of your friends and watch their shoulders droop when they talk about their retirement funds vaporizing in some mutual fund. When done properly [real estate has the] best consistent rates of return with [the] least risk of any of the readily available investment options.

—Harold Line

## Investing for the Future

No one will care about your future like you will. Create a legacy to leave for your future generations.

—Kris F.

It is said that if you give a man a fish, he will eat for a day. If you teach a man to fish, he will eat in perpetuity. In that same vein, I look forward to imparting the same distilled wisdom and experience I have gleaned to my children so that they may prosper and share this with their future generations!

—Scott Crawford

Not only does it create wealth in my lifetime, but it is wealth that will be transferred into my children's lives and future generations. It allows me to bless others along the way.

—Nelson Camp

## Power of Leverage

Start making money work for you; work smarter not harder.

—Jarrett Brian Vaughan

Real estate is *real!* Real people pay real money every month in a real asset that is their real home. And thus real valuations based on real cash flow after real operating expenses can be easily obtained with real equity created through real mortgage paydown and real value appreciation! It is a very social asset with inflation-protected rents and values, where valuations are far tougher to manipulate than the stock market. Income for life with rising equity. Seems like a no-brainer to me.

—Thomas Beyer

## Superior Market Class

While equity markets go up and down, real estate has proven to be the most reliable hedge

*(continued)*

against inflation—superior to all other asset classes. It represents the last predictable and reliable cash flow mechanism in the world [and] you don't have to count on the ethics of top corporate executives to achieve [success].

—Calum Ross

[It's been] proven time and time again that real estate is the best way to increase your wealth.

1. It allows you to (safely) use the banks' money to invest.
2. You can then make improvements and changes to add value.
3. Options: live in it, rent it, flip it, lease it, leverage it, borrow against it, re-zone it, subdivide it...

—Rob Patenaude

You have the control. When you purchase stocks, there is nothing you can do to make them increase.

—Glen Godlonton

Real estate is a safe asset over long-term. It pays all through its maturing process and pays extremely well at the end when you offer it to another to do the same (investor), or you provide a family with a home.

I like to sleep well at night and I'm not worried about the economic world coming to an end. I have chosen my locations under heavy scrutiny where they will always be in high demand. People always need a place to live. I have zero worries about my investments crashing.

—Nelson Camp

## Cash Flow

Cash flow provides choices.

—Don R. Campbell

With a proper system and due diligence, the returns are predictable and replicable.

—Dineen Jogola

Cash flow, mortgage paydown and leverage in strong markets provide excellent returns for investors and you have more control in locating these regions and individual properties than you typically have when investing in stocks and bonds.

—Mitch Collins

*(continued)*

## Learn-able, Doable

> Due diligence on properties is fairly simple,
> easier to reduce the risk on a potential property.
> —Marty Green

Another great aspect of real estate investing is
that it rewards knowledge. One has to look at an
area and *learn* everything he/she can about the
area's past, present and future. Many other investment vehicles reward risk tolerance and risk
management. Instead of concentrating on one
thing in an effort to acquire useful knowledge,
one needs to diversify in order to minimize risk.

Gaining knowledge is more noble and effective than increasing one's risk tolerance.

> —Sam Hosseini

Because you can. No matter age, health, income,
credit…you can.

> —Corey Young

First things that come to mind: versatility, time
and tangibility. Having various investments
in my portfolio and watching performance of
each. What I love about real estate is having a
property and watching the equity grow. Buy and

hold. The more the mortgage is paid off—rental rates increase—more cash flow for me.

Time is precious as we all know. Watching stock, financial reports seems like a gamble and [it's] time-consuming. While I'm retired, sitting on a beach, I'm making money. More stability to support my lifestyle . . . Not sitting there worried and having to make a call to a stockbroker or [anticipate a] potential crash.

Tangible—being kind of a control freak, it's nice to be able to see it and touch it. [I like being] in control of what I buy and doing my own analysis. [If it] doesn't work—move on.

—Shannon P. Murree

## Great People

A less technical answer: You get to meet so many great people!

—Andrew C. MacDonald

Because it's the most fun you'll ever have while learning and earning.

—Heather Grief Vickar

# About the Author

———— ❧ ————

Don R. Campbell is the Senior Analyst of the Real Estate Investment Network (REIN™), whose membership exceeds 3,400 successful Canadian real estate investors with a combined portfolio that tops $4 billion in residential real estate.

Don is an active real estate investor who teaches proven real estate investment strategies at live workshops held across the country. He is the author of the Canadian bestseller *Real Estate Investing in Canada 2.0*, a book that all real estate investors should have as an action tool and reference. A popular real estate commentator in private and public media, Don has also co-authored several other real estate investment books, where he shares his market and investment research alongside years of his own hands-on experience.

In addition to helping countless investors achieve their dreams, Don and fellow REIN members have raised more than $900,000 for charities such as Habitat for Humanity. To tap into Don's experience and learn more about his workshops, visit www.DonRCampbell.com, or follow his updates on Twitter @donrcampbell or on Facebook as theREINman.